"It might make one in love with death, to think that one should be buried in so sweet a place."

—Percy Bysshe Shelley

A MORTAL'S GUIDE TO CEMETERIES

Amanda R. Woomer

(A Mortal's Guide to Cemeteries: A Morbid Activity Book for the Blossoming Taphophile)

Original Cover Artwork Designed by

ISBN 979-8-866-95131-4

Printed in USA by Spook-Eats Publishing

FOR GRAMMA AW,
WHO USED TO TAKE ME ON WALKS THROUGH THE LOCAL CEMETERY.

OTHER TITLES BY AMANDA R. WOOMER

The Art of Grieving

A Very Frightful Victorian Christmas

THE SPIRIT GUIDE SERIES:
America's Haunted Breweries, Distilleries, and Wineries
Harlots & Hauntings

THE FEMININE MACABRE:
A Woman's Journal of All Things Strange & Unusual
The Feminine Macabre Volume II
The Feminine Macabre Volume III
The Feminine Macabre Volume IV
The Feminine Macabre Volume V

A Haunted Atlas of Western New York

The Ghosts of the Ghostlight Theatre

Hell Hath No Fury 3 with Troy Taylor

A Teen's Guide to Ghost Hunting

CREEPY BOOKS FOR CREEPY KIDS:
The Cryptid ABC Book
Krampus's Great Big Book of Yuletide Monsters
A Child's Guide to Cemeteries

A Mortal's Guide to Cemeteries

Amanda R. Woomer

CONTENTS

INTRODUCTION

One of my favorite childhood memories was when my Gramma Aw took me and my cousins to the most famous cemetery in Buffalo, New York: Forest Lawn Cemetery. An artist to her core, she would excitedly point out the undeniable craftsmanship on all of the graves, ranging from the stunning monuments and mausoleums to the simpler (but no less beautiful) graves scattered along the paths and waterways. I still don't know how my cousins felt about these macabre field trips, but I absolutely loved them, and I've continued going on them even though my grandmother has been dead for almost seven years now.

If I'm being honest with myself, the reason I am my melancholy (slightly morbid) self is because of my grandmother. I consider her one of my soul mates, and I knew it was only a matter of time before I finally sat down and wrote a book focused on one of my (and her) favorite subjects: cemeteries.

The sadhus (holy men) at Pashupatinath shortly after the Hindu funeral.

For me, there has always been something strangely comforting about cemeteries. As a child, I crossed my fingers and held my breath each time we drove past one. They were the settings for scary stories we told at slumber parties or around campfires, but over time (probably thanks to my

gramma), I fell in love with them. While living and traveling abroad, I acquainted myself with death and the numerous mourning customs found around the world, including exploring the Imperial Crypt in Vienna, Austria, where my idol Elisabeth of Bavaria (lovingly known as Sisi) is interred, witnessing a Hindu funeral in Pashupatinath Temple in Kathmandu, Nepal, and even holding William Burke's death mask in the Edinburgh Vaults in Scotland. After my brother died in 2015 at just 19 years old, I found my morbid curiosity involving death taking on a new life, leading me to start The Traveling Museum of Memento Mori and slap a bumper sticker on my car that reads I BRAKE FOR CEMETERIES. In my heart, I knew I wanted to try to find ways to make death not nearly as scary as society has conditioned us to believe.

During the COVID-19 pandemic, I took my son on walks through the cemetery at the end of my street—similar to a park, I knew there wouldn't be anyone else weird enough to be there, so I felt comfortable taking him somewhere outside that he could run around and play. While researching this book, he remained my cemetery buddy. While he's still only three years old (and an energetic three at that), I've taken the time to try to teach him what he can and cannot do in a cemetery, what certain things mean, and have even tried to make a game out of finding certain symbols on the graves.

Knowing how much I enjoyed exploring these places as a young girl and watching my son do the same thing, I knew I needed to create two versions of this book: *A Mortal's Guide to Cemeteries* and *A Child's Guide to Cemeteries*. Both versions introduce the readers to things they might see in the graveyard while also offering them ways to respectfully interact with the dead with whom they might come into contact. I hope you're able to use these books as not only a way to connect with the dead but the living as well. May these macabre activity books help prepare you for the inevitability that is to come… and help you make memories in the meantime.

Amanda

November 2023

AN IMPORTANT NOTE

Please note that this book discusses various topics surrounding death that some readers may find disturbing, including the death of children and images of human remains. Discretion is advised.

Keep in mind that you must show respect to every cemetery you visit while exploring with this book. Please adhere to all rules, including the hours of operation. It is debatable whether gravestone rubbing is ethical, given the delicate state of so many graves and the damage numerous rubbings can cause. In fact, many cemeteries prohibit gravestone rubbings. Remember that all graves are sacred whether the cemetery hasn't been used in centuries or is still the site of active funerals. Respect is everything when exploring cemeteries.

We have also blurred any sensitive information on the graves featured in this book, including names, dates, and some locations out of respect for the dead and the living loved ones they left behind. Out of fear of vandalism, we have also chosen not to disclose where the images in this book were taken.

A MORTAL'S GUIDE TO CEMETERIES

Amanda R. Woomer

PART ONE
CEMETERY HISTORY

HISTORY OF HUMAN BURIAL

It is said that death is the great equalizer. Anything that once separated humans by class, race, sex, or religion is seemingly wiped away when someone breathes their final breath. However, death and the eventual funeral and burial that follows seem to come in various forms throughout history and even in the 21st Century.

Burial is seen as not only a way to show respect to the dead but also as a way to provide closure for the family and to keep them from witnessing the decomposition process. In many instances, it was (and still is) seen as a way for the individual to successfully enter the afterlife. Due to this belief, burial has become one of the most ritualized aspects of one's life, with numerous ways to assist in the process of burial, including mummification, sea burials, cremation, embalming, and natural or green burials that are becoming exceedingly popular in recent years.

FUN FACT: Edgar Allan Poe's story *The Premature Burial* led to a widespread fear of being buried alive.

Evidence suggests that 130,000 years ago, the now-extinct early human group, the Neanderthals, were among the first to intentionally bury their dead. Along with burying their dead in shallow graves, Neanderthals were also known to add grave goods such as tools and animal bones. According to some researchers, such a practice is one of the earliest signs of faith in an afterlife, with the living providing the dead with things they might need.

Special attention was given to what awaited the deceased after death in almost every culture in the ancient world:

In Ancient Greece, women would tend to the bodies, ensuring that they placed a coin (or "obol") on or inside the corpse's mouth. This was known as Charon's obol and would be used as payment for the ferryman, Charon, who would take the souls of the dead across the rivers Acheron and Styx, separating the world of the living from the Underworld.

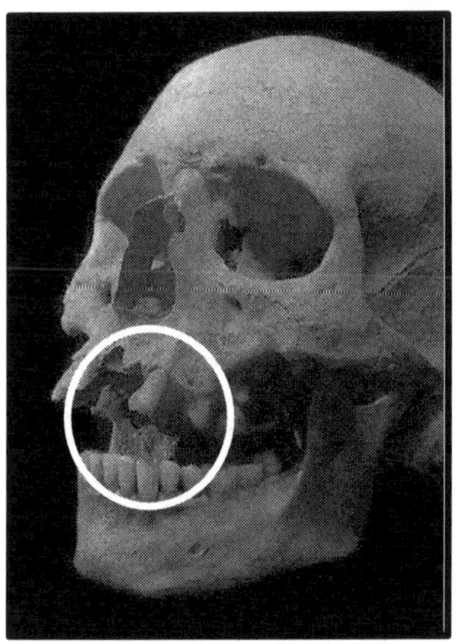

A skull with an obol in the mouth from the Prehistory Museum of Valencia
Photo courtesy of Falconaumanni

In Ancient Rome, it was believed that if an individual died unnaturally ("before their natural term") or their family failed to perform the appropriate funeral rites, the spirit would haunt the living as vengeful ghosts known as lemures.

The first emperor of China, Qin Shi Huang, was buried between 210 and 209 BCE with 8,000 terracotta soldiers, 130 chariots with 520 horses, and an additional 150 calvary horses.

What we now refer to as the Terracotta Army was created to protect the emperor in the afterlife.

A small portion of the Terracotta Army.
Author's personal photo

However, more than any other ancient group, the Egyptians are remembered for their elaborate burial customs that have fascinated the general public for centuries. Unlike their contemporaries, the Egyptians refused to cremate their dead, instead preserving the bodies that would be needed in the afterlife, believing it ensured immortality. While not everyone in Ancient Egypt was mummified, as it was a long and expensive process, most burials did include casting spells and burying the dead with specific grave goods intended to be used in the afterlife. Grave goods in Egypt evolved significantly from the animal bones of the Late Pleistocene Era. Instead, Ancient Egyptians might have been buried with furniture, games, and food. In many cases, men were buried with weapons, while women were buried with makeup palettes. During the First Dynasty (c.3100-2900 BCE), the servants of both high court nobility and pharaohs would be killed and buried with the deceased in order to continue serving them in death. Eventually, the practice of retainer sacrifice ended, and the corpses of actual servants were replaced with shabti figures still intended to serve their master in the afterlife.

An antechamber of King Tutankhamun's tomb included funeral flowers, a painted chest filled with royal robes and jewels, a long box containing the king's underwear, and a ceremonial couch.

By the Middle Ages, interment became the widely accepted form of burial in Europe, with death (thanks to famine, disease, and war) being a universally common part of life. The average lifespan for a man in 1276 was only 31 years (much different from the 21st Century's average of 77 years). As we'll see from later generations, the idea of a "good death" was crucial to the grieving process, no matter the era in which an individual lived. For those who experienced death in the Middle Ages, having the individual prepared to meet their Creator surrounded by friends and family at home while a priest performed the last rites was the ideal way to die. However, the "good death" was not available to everyone from 1347 to 1353 when the Black Plague swept through Europe, killing between 75 and 200 million people. Because of the disease's contagiousness, no one was willing to go near the sick, so many died without hearing their last rites. Bodies were piled on carts before being brought to mass graves for burial. Just 300 years later, the bubonic plague returned to London with a vengeance. Between 1665 and 1666, the Great Plague of London killed at least 68,000 Londoners (with some estimating the actual number was closer to 100,000). It should be noted that one of our misconceptions about burial stems directly from this particular plague. Today, it's believed that graves are buried six feet deep (thanks to the expression "six feet under" to denote that someone is dead). However, there is no universal measurement for a grave, and most are not dug quite that deep unless another body is intended to be buried on top of it. The expression comes from John Lawrence, the Lord Mayor of London at the time of the Great Plague, who ordered, "...all the Graves shall be at least six foot deep."

FUN FACT: According to the World Health Organization technically only corpses carrying infectious diseases need to be buried.

The concept of a "good death" was tested again during the Victorian Era, particularly during the American Civil War (1861-

1865). At this point in American history, child mortality rates were dropping, and if a child made it to their fifth birthday, they were expected to live until middle age. However, with the onslaught of the Civil War, hundreds of thousands of young men died violently. They were not surrounded by friends and family in the safety of their home after living a long life. In many instances, they died afraid, alone, and anonymous, as many soldiers went unidentified.

"Bloody Lane" in the sunken road after the Battle of Antietam, 1862.
Photo by Alexander Gardner

One of the most unexpected problems of the war became disposing of the dead. Although commanding officers on both sides of the conflict were ordered to bury their dead with the honor expected in the Christian faith, the undesirable duty often fell to locals or prisoners of war, who were rarely equipped with wagons or even shovels.

At the start of the war, soldiers are recorded as being appalled that the opposing army didn't return to the battlefield to tend to their dead. Over time, it was clear that the needs of the surviving soldiers were far more important than taking care of the dead, resulting in the defeated party retreating and the victor being responsible for disposing of the bodies. Because of this, there are instances of burials lacking the adequate manpower, dignity, and respect ideal for a burial.

Many soldiers were buried in unmarked mass graves, hopefully dug deep enough to keep scavengers—be they thieves or animals—away from the bodies. However, more often than not, the weather or wild animals would reveal the decaying bodies buried in shallow trenches. Often, soldiers were buried naked or in their underwear—their comrades or thieves would often take what they needed, such as clothes, weapons, and supplies, from the bodies—making it almost impossible to identify the individual.

As if robbing from the dead and bodies popping up from their graves wasn't horrific enough for the grieving families that once hoped for a good death for their loved ones, there was also the very dire matter of how long it took the living to inter the dead.

> *The weather was phenomenally hot, and the stench from the hundreds of black, bloated, decomposed, maggoty bodies, exposed to a torrid heat for three days after the battle was a sight truly*

horrid, and beggaring all power of verbal expression... Just over there in Mumma's field in one ditch you placed 185 Confederate corpses, the one on top of the other, and indecorously covered them from sight with clay. In other ditches lesser numbers were similarly buried. Time and circumstances forbade a more humane course than this.

-S. M. Whistler
Company E
130th Pennsylvania
Battle of Antietam

The violent deaths experienced by these young men and the impersonal burials reshaped the way Americans viewed death and how the government responded to it.

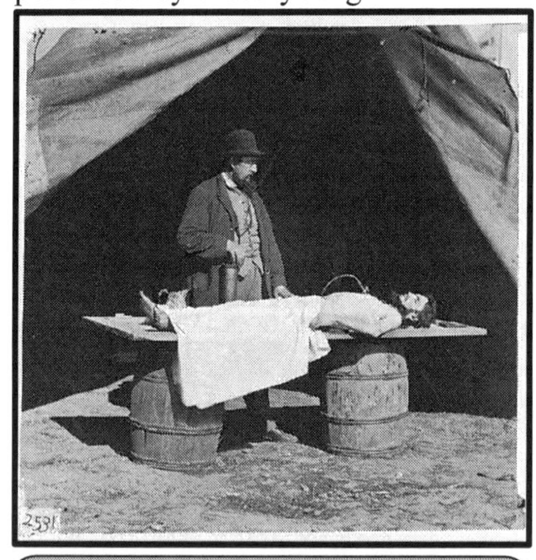

Dr. Richard Burr, an embalming surgeon demonstrating the procedure on a dead soldier.
LC-DIG-cwpb-01887

Several Northern states declared that they would bring every slain soldier home at the onset of the war. However, this quickly became too large of a task, so families took it upon themselves to track down their kin.

Some wealthy families were able to travel to the battlefields themselves to find their loved ones. At the same time, others hired embalmers at $100 ($2,390 today) per body to preserve their family members before also paying for metal caskets and refrigeration to transport the soldier home. However, these were privileges designated for the wealthy, so many families never learned what truly happened to their fathers, brothers, husbands, and sons.

> **FUN FACT:** After his assassination, Abraham Lincoln's body went on a 20-day tour from Washington, D.C. to Springfield, IL, stopping in 10 cities. This was only possible because his body had been embalmed.

Private organizations and the Sanitary Commission helped bring Union soldiers home, providing services such as the disinterment of the body, embalming, metal caskets, and shipping costs. Of course, the Sanitary Commission was not always available. Often, families relied on private embalmers and undertakers who followed the armies and managed to build successful businesses helping mourning families bring their brave young men home.

The Civil War changed American's views on death and funeral customs and made embalming a common practice to help slow the decaying process. Despite its popularity (and necessity) during the Civil War, embalming has existed for millennia in one form or another (one extreme example is mummification) found among the Aztecs, Mayans, Tibetan

> **FUN FACT:** Lord Nelson's body was preserved for two months in 1805 in a mixture of brandy and myrrh while on board the *Victory* before being returned to England.

tribes, the Guanches, and the Ancient Egyptians and Chinese. Attempts at persevering bodies were made throughout the Middle Ages and Renaissance in Europe, with the earliest attempt to inject the vascular system dating to the 14th Century (even Leonardo da Vinci attempted to perfect his own process). Modern embalming techniques as we know them today were developed by Scottish surgeon William Hunter in the late 18th Century, making ice packing and cooling boards obsolete.

Today, embalming allows families to view the deceased one last time without being subjected to the effects of decomposition, which can be disturbing to some.

> **FUN FACT:** Have you ever noticed rocks on a grave? It is a Jewish tradition to leave a rock instead of flowers when you visit a grave because flowers die but rocks last forever (like our love).

It's important to note that embalming is not the only option available. Traditional Jewish law forbids embalming, requiring that the corpse be buried as quickly as possible. Those who practice Hinduism will be cremated usually within 24 hours of death. Natural burials or green burials have become exceedingly popular since the 1990s, where the body is placed in the ground (either in a biodegradable shroud or a wicker basket) to decompose back into the earth naturally. According to the Cremation Association of North America, 56% of Americans who died in 2020 chose to be cremated, making it more popular than traditional burial. Other unique burial options in recent years include memorial coral reefs and tree pods. However, it's important to note that no legislation currently protects these burial sites. Sky burial is a rare practice outside of Tibet, where human remains are left on mountaintops to be eaten by scavenging animals, ultimately returning the individual to nature. Another custom that seems unusual (and possibly even disturbing to some) is cannibalizing the flesh or ground-up bones of the deceased as a form of mourning. This form of endocannibalism has been seen in the ancient Callatiae tribe in India and among various Indigenous groups in Brazil and Peru, the Jukun people of Nigeria, and the Fore people of Papua New Guinea.

A corpse being carried from Lhasa for sky burial, the corpse is sewn into a yak hair cloth and two white silk Khata as offerings, c.1920.

No matter how we choose to dispose of the dead, one unifying factor across the centuries, as well as cultures, has been the desire to show the individual one last sign of respect as they transition from this life to whatever might come next.

TYPES OF CEMETERIES

While burying human remains has been part of our history for over 100,000 years, relegating a specific area to communally bury our dead is a relatively new concept.

The word "cemetery" comes from the Greek word *koimeterion*, meaning "sleeping place," and is land specifically set aside for the burial of the dead. Perhaps one of the oldest known cemeteries is Gross Fredenwalde Cemetery, just one hour north of Berlin. This particular cemetery dates back 8,500 years and is the final resting place of at least 11 Mesolithic individuals, purposefully buried together. Such an archaeological discovery is extremely rare since their hunter-gatherer lifestyle made them nomadic.

The royal burial mounds of Gamla Uppsala, Sweden.

As discussed in the previous chapter, burial practices differed worldwide, ranging from cremation to burial and even cannibalism. In instances with burial and cremation, often, people sought a place to inter the remains. These ancient locations might come in the form of burial mounds (as seen all over the world, including parts of Africa, Asia, the Middle East, all across Europe, and North and South America), grave fields of Northern Europe and Scandinavia, and necropolises found in Ancient Egypt, Greece, and Persia.

By the 7th Century, burials in Europe came under the Church's jurisdiction and would take place on the consecrated grounds of the church. The area of the churchyard designated for burial was known as a graveyard. Churches were often situated within communities, making space limited. As time passed and more people died, graveyards became overcrowded, and the configuration of the graves became chaotic as space continued to fill in. Often, bodies were buried one on top of the other. Eventually, serious concerns for the health and safety of those living near the churchyards led to the creation of new cemeteries outside the cities.

Charter Street Cemetery, Salem, MA.

RURAL CEMETERIES

Also sometimes known as garden cemeteries, these new places of burial reflected the changing opinion of death and the afterlife in the 18th and 19th Centuries. No longer viewing death in a harsh way as their ancestors had in Europe and Colonial America, the use of expansive park-like settings complete with trees, flowers, and ponds was a way to make death more approachable and possibly even beautiful. In addition to this softer view of death, rural cemeteries were also a solution to the sudden increase in population at the start of the Industrial Revolution. As people migrated to cities in search of jobs and the population grew denser, space in graveyards grew even more limited, and the spread of yellow fever among those living near the churchyards was cause for concern. Additionally, prior to the popularity of embalming, the smell of rotting flesh hung heavy in the air

Greyfriars Kirkyard in Edinburgh, Scotland, shows how close civilians lived to graveyards.

in urban centers, leading government officials to seek an alternative.

English architect, astronomer, and mathematician Sir Christopher Wren advocated for burial grounds outside the city as early as 1711. His plan called for a burial place on the outskirts of town "inclosed with a strong Brick Wall, and having a Walk round, and two cross Walks, decently planted with Yew-trees… where the Dead need not be disturbed… or piled four or five upon one another, or Bones thrown out to gain Room."

It would be nearly a century before the first rural cemetery, Père Lachaise Cemetery, would open in Paris in 1804. Established by Napoleon, who had been named emperor just three days prior, he declared that every citizen had the right to be buried regardless

Early 20th Century postcard of Père Lachaise Cemetery.

of race or religion. Notable figures buried here include Chopin, Marcel Proust, Georges Méliès, Oscar Wilde, and Jim Morrison.

The first rural cemetery established in the United States was Mount Auburn Cemetery in Cambridge, Massachusetts, in 1831. In the 1840s, Mount Auburn was considered one of the most popular tourist destinations alongside Niagara Falls.

Before public parks, rural cemeteries were the places where the general public could go for outdoor recreation (once reserved solely for the very wealthy). Such activities included strolling along the winding paths among the graves, monuments, and mausoleums, reading, and even enjoying a picnic with friends or family.

Built anywhere from one to five miles from the city center (far enough from the general population but close enough to visit), over 100 rural cemeteries were established throughout the 19th Century in the United States.

In 1847, the New York State Legislature passed the Rural Cemetery Act, which authorized the commercialization of burial grounds, successfully removing the Church's control over funerals and burials. Many rural cemeteries were no longer sectarian, meaning different groups could finally be buried together.

Sadly, the cost of maintaining such expansive cemeteries with elaborate monuments became too expensive, and soon, only the wealthy could afford to be interred within these new burial grounds. This led to a counter-culture at the end of the 19th Century and the birth of a new type of cemetery.

LAWN CEMETERY

As the name might suggest, these cemeteries are covered in grass with name plaques embedded in the ground, creating a lawn-like appearance. This new design was introduced by Adolph Strauch in Cincinnati in 1855 and was quickly embraced by the middle class. Unlike rural cemeteries incorporating rolling hills and waterways, these are relatively flat, making maintenance easy and cheap.

The author's grandmother is buried in a lawn cemetery.

One of the disadvantages of lawn cemeteries is the opportunity for grass to grow over the plaques, making them difficult to locate or read. Often, tokens of affection such as flowers, small gifts, or toys are not permitted at the gravesites as they inhibit maintenance.

Today, lawn beam cemeteries are trying to solve the issue of invasive plant growth. These raised concrete slabs/beams run along the rows of graves with the plaques resting on top of them, still creating a lawn appearance.

COLUMBARIUM

Columbarium walls are often a tiny part of a much larger cemetery, with more being constructed in recent years with the continued increase in cremation's popularity. While some families choose to keep one's cremated remains at home in an urn, others prefer to have an established permanent public place where friends and loved ones can still visit, pay their respects, and mourn. These walls are often made of brick with small rectangular niches just large enough to store the cremated remains of an individual. This type of cemetery is popular where space is limited, such as in Japan, where cremation is mandatory in most of the country. Burial in a columbarium wall is also significantly cheaper than a burial plot (which would also require a casket and vault in the United States).

FUN FACT: The term comes from the Latin word *columba* and originally only referred to the compartments doves and pigeons lived in.

In ancient times, columbariums were built partially or entirely underground. Today, they may be free-standing structures, part of a mausoleum, or you may find a columbarium wall inside a church such as the Cathedral of Our Lady of the Angels in Los Angeles. You'll also find such cemeteries outside of Western culture, particularly in Buddhist temples such as *naguta* ("bone receiving pagodas") in China and *nōkotsudō* ("bone receiving halls") in Japan. Both of these structures are public spaces that allow families to visit and practice ancestor rites.

Columbarium at Père Lachaise Cemetery.
Photo courtesy of Pierre-Yves Beaudouin

Columbarium wall (left) and columbarium at Manila's Thousand Buddha Temple (right).
Photo courtesy of Kerry Raymond and Zarate123

OSSUARY

As previously mentioned regarding early Christian burials, space in churchyards was extremely limited, with bodies often piled on top of one another. One solution to the ever-increasing number of bodies and the limited space available within graveyards was an ossuary.

Technically, anything can be an ossuary—a box, a container, a room, and even a building that acts as the final resting place of one's skeletal remains. Those of the lower classes would often be buried in temporary mass graves and eventually exhumed years later to make space for the newly deceased. Even individual graves were often dug up, and the skeletal remains removed to offer space

The Sedlec Ossuary contains the remains of at least 40,000 people.
Photo courtesy of Interfase

for newer corpses that needed a place to decompose. The skeletons would then be brought to their final resting place, where countless others would join them.

The act of combining skeletal remains into a single area to save on space dates back at least 3,000 years to Ancient Persia.

One of the most famous ossuaries is the Sedlec Ossuary in the Czech Republic, while the Douaumont Ossuary in France is a modern ossuary containing the remains of over 130,000 French and German soldiers from the Battle of Verdun in World War I.

FUN FACT: According to legend, the unpleasant task of exhuming the human remains and stacking their bones in the chapel of Sedlec Ossuary was given to a half-blind monk in 1511.

The world's largest ossuary is found beneath the streets of Paris in the Paris Catacombs. Spanning over 190 miles of tunnels, over six million people are buried there. With the words *Arrête! C'est ici l'empire de la Mort* ("Stop! This is the empire of Death") written above the entrance, the Paris Catacombs have been a tourist attraction almost since their inception.

While the idea of removing an individual's remains from one place to another may seem macabre by our standards today, at a time in human history when space was limited and mortality rates were exceptionally high, it simply made sense—one could fit far more skeletal remains than coffins into a single tomb.

Today, ossuaries seemingly overcrowded with skeletal remains of humans from centuries ago sitting out in the open manage to both repel and fascinate us.

A column of human bones found in the Paris Catacombs. Photo courtesy of Amanda D. Paulson

Several human skeletons within the Paris Catacombs. Photo courtesy of Amy & Ryan's Weird Adventures

An engraving from 1855 depicting the catacombs as a tourist attraction.

Photo courtesy of Amy & Ryan's Weird Adventures

PET CEMETERIES

Perhaps the only cemetery more peculiar than an ossuary is a pet cemetery.

For most of human history, people have had pets, and when their beloved cats and dogs have died, they've managed to find ways to honor their passing just as they would with their own family members.

The world's oldest known pet cemetery was just discovered in 2011 during the excavation of the Berenice Troglodytica seaport in Egypt on the Red Sea. Unsurprisingly, most of the animals that were buried here were cats that were mummified and honored, as the Ancient Egyptians viewed them as deities.

Mummified cat, Ancient Egypt, 2000-100 BCE.
Photo courtesy of Science Museum, London, Wellcome Images L0057093

Evidence shows that humans and their dogs were buried side by side in Siberia over 8,000 years ago.

The Ashkelon dog cemetery in Israel is the final resting place of thousands of dogs buried between the 5th and 3rd Centuries BCE.

The Hyde Park pet cemetery was an informal cemetery in the gatekeeper's garden from 1881 to 1903. Over 300 pets were buried there, complete with tiny tombstones.

Hyde Park's makeshift pet cemetery.
Photo courtesy of JRennocks

The first pet cemetery in the United States was Hartsdale Pet Cemetery, which opened in 1896 in Hartsdale, New York. Today, it is the largest pet cemetery in the country, with over 70,000 animals buried here, including Ming the tiger.

Today, cemeteries are beginning to allow humans and domesticated animals to be buried side by side, which may ultimately lead to the end of pet cemeteries.

UNIQUE GRAVES

It's easy to get lost as you wander through cemeteries, no matter the type or size. These are just a few of the unique things you should keep an eye out for when exploring your local cemeteries.

ZINKER

These unique gravestones are easy to spot once you know what to look for. Originally referred to as "white bronze" by manufacturers (even though they were not made of bronze), today, they are known as "zinkers" due to the zinc they are constructed from. When first cast, these monuments were white, but over time, they took on a bluish hue, making it extremely easy to spot them in a sea of marble and granite tombstones.

First introduced to the American public in the 1870s, zinkers experienced a somewhat short-lived popularity, eventually dying out by the early 20th Century. Sold in newspapers, catalogs, and through traveling salesmen, zinkers provided elaborate monuments at an affordable price for members of the growing middle class. The most common shape was a four-sided obelisk, which allowed each side to be personalized with various symbols for the individual or the family it commemorated. Despite their affordability, these graves were seen as cheap and tacky and quickly fell out of style. Ironically, these "tacky" graves are some of the best-preserved ones you might come across.

Keep your eye out for a blue or bluish-gray monument or grave marker. These graves are also hollow, so gently tap them to ensure you've found a zinker. You'll also notice the very large screws (that almost resemble acorns) and the seams in each corner.

Hopkinsville Kentuckian, *July 7, 1899.*

MORTSAFE

Every few months, a photo of a mortsafe makes its rounds on the internet, claiming to be evidence of people's belief in vampires or zombies throughout history. While belief in supernatural beings is a conversation for another day, cages placed on top of graves were a common feature in cemeteries in the United Kingdom during the 19th Century.

Resurrection men (also referred to as body snatchers) supplied anatomists and surgeons with cadavers starting in the 18th Century. While today we can say we've benefitted from such dastardly deeds, during the 18th and 19th Centuries, families were genuinely concerned that body snatchers would dig up the remains of their deceased loved ones to be dissected and studied. While the desecration of a grave was enough to shock any devout Christian at the time, police and city officials often turned a blind eye. They kept publicity off the resurrection men as they knew medical students needed to study and better understand the human body to advance science and medicine. Unfortunately, it was a necessary evil.

FUN FACT: Burke and Hare are often remembered as the most successful body snatchers. However, they never removed a body from the ground, instead, they killed at least 16 people and sold the bodies. Ironically Burke was executed and dissected in the anatomy theatre of Edinburgh's Old College.

The mortsafe was invented around 1816 to solve the growing problem of body snatchers. While wealthy families could afford precautions such as vaults and mausoleums, mortsafes could be rented to a family for the first six weeks after a loved one's death.

Photo courtesy of Darren and Jessica Cooke

By then, the bodies would have decayed to the point where the surgeons would no longer want the bodies, and the mortsafe could be removed and rented to someone else.

Because of their disposable nature, as the threat of body snatchers fell, so too did the need for mortsafes. They are extremely rare in the United States (according to Find A Grave, there are only two). If you're hoping to find one, you'll need to travel to the United Kingdom, particularly Scotland.

FIELDSTONE

If you're ever wandering through an old countryside cemetery and stumble on what looks like a simple rock, take a closer look because you might have found a fieldstone.

FUN FACT: An epitaph is anything written on a grave aside from one's name and dates such as "Rest in Peace." There are some unique epitaphs out there, so keep an eye out!

Much like today, the death industry often tries to find ways to make money, and one of the most common ways throughout history was with gravestones. While some families could afford beautiful grave markers filled with symbolism and long epitaphs, poorer families were not so lucky. However, instead of leaving the dead in an unmarked grave, they would take a stone from the surrounding landscape and use it as a makeshift marker, often filing it to resemble a gravestone.

Photo courtesy of @cemetery_dryad

If there was any crude inscription, it has long since vanished, thanks to the elements. However, the vast majority of fieldstones had no markings on them.

Despite their simple appearance, these stones should be viewed with the same amount of respect as an elaborate grave, as just as much love would have gone into these fieldstones.

CENOTAPH

A cenotaph is a memorial erected for an individual buried somewhere else or whose remains were never recovered. The name comes from the Ancient Greek word *kenotaphion* with *kenos* meaning "empty" and *taphos* meaning "tomb." While these are often constructed for fallen soldiers, cenotaphs can be in memory of anyone and can come in different shapes and sizes, ranging from plaques and benches to mausoleums and monuments. These unique structures can be found in cemeteries, however, you might also find them in public parks. No matter where you find a cenotaph, they all act as a place where people can go to pay their respects. Some famous cenotaphs include the original grave of Edgar Allan Poe, where he was buried from 1849 to 1875, the stone arch cenotaph at the Hiroshima Peace Memorial Park in honor of those who lost their lives to the atomic bomb in 1945, London's Whitehall Cenotaph to honor the dead from World War I and World War II, a cenotaph for those who died defending the Alamo which is erected in front of the Alamo Mission Chapel, and the cenotaph for Ida and Isidor Straus (owner of the department store Macy's) who both perished when the *RMS Titanic* sank in 1912. While Isidor's body was recovered, Ida's was not so her family took water from the wreck site and placed it in the Straus Mausoleum with the words on the cenotaph reading, *Many waters cannot quench love—neither can the floods drown it* (Song of Solomon 8:7).

Photo courtesy of KRichter

17TH AND 18TH CENTURY GRAVE FEATURES

Some of the most common graves you'll find in New England are filled with symbols specific to certain sections of the grave, including the border, finial, and tympanum. You'll find examples of the artwork unique to each area throughout this book.

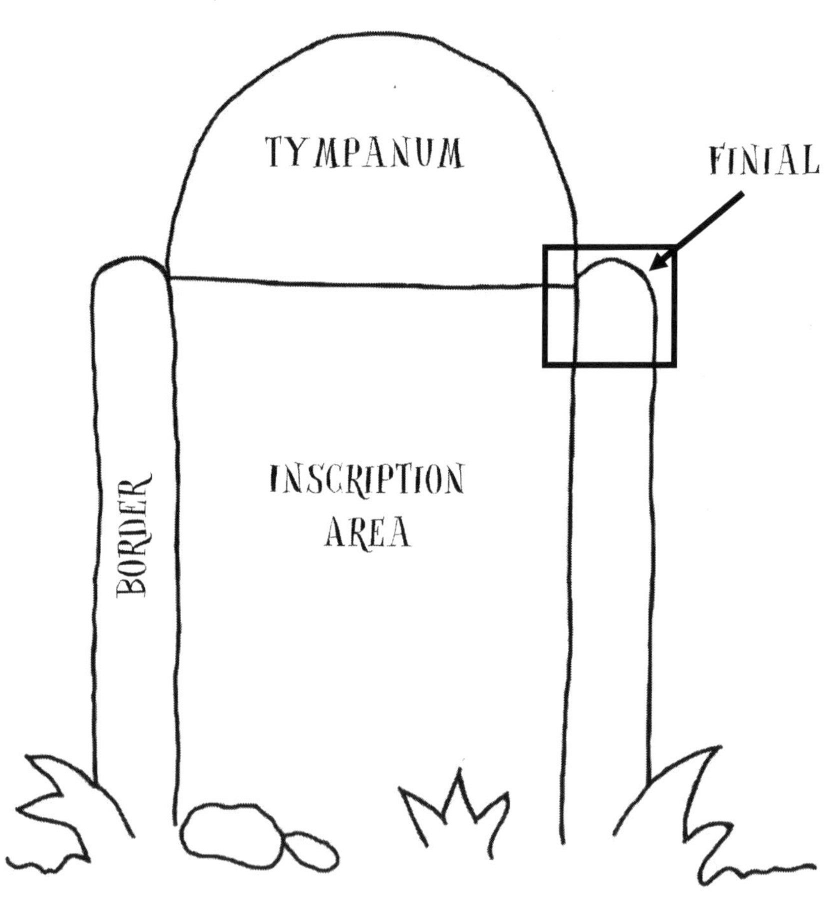

PART TWO
CEMETERY SYMBOLISM

CEMETERY SYMBOLISM

Cemeteries are stunning locations without knowing the secret language of the tombstones. The moment you understand the meaning behind the various images carved onto the graves, a whole new world opens up for you. We've compiled a list of the numerous symbols you might see while wandering through a cemetery, including flowers, animals, images denoting one's occupation, marriage status, and even some morbid symbolism. We encourage you to bring this book with you every time you find yourself in a cemetery to help decode the messages hidden in the stones.

Charter Street Cemetery, Salem, MA.

FLOWERS

Acorns and oak leaves: acorns represent humble beginnings, patience, and faith, while oak leaves symbolize strength and stability. The acorn itself is a small and unassuming seed. However, it holds the potential to grow into one of the strongest trees in the forest.

Photo courtesy of @cemetery_dryad

Bud: the death of a child. Often shown bent or broken to represent a life cut short.

The grave of a brother and sister who died in 1832 and 1845 represented by the two bent buds.

Calla lily: most often representative of marriage. They can also symbolize resurrection as they bloom around Easter and resemble a trumpet, which would be used to spread the Christian "good news."

Corn: could denote that the interred was a farmer in life. The corn kernel also represents rebirth. Like wheat and grapes, it can also mean a long life as corn is harvested after a successful season (in the case of the deceased, a long life).

The epitaph reads "As a shock of corn in his season" referencing Job 5:26 in the Bible. In this case, the corn likely symbolizes a long life as the reverend was 89 years old.

Daisy: the death of a child. In the Victorian language of flowers, daisies could symbolize innocence. They can also represent purity and new beginnings.

Daffodil: rebirth and resurrection. Also known as narcissus, it is said to be the flower of the Underworld, growing along the banks of the River Styx.

Fern: sincerity, humility, and solitude due to the fact that they live on the forest floor and have remained unchanged for millions of years, found all over the planet.

Forget-me-not: remembrance, eternal love, and faithfulness. Originates from the 15th Century and by the 19th Century, was a symbol of love.

Grapes: a cluster could mean someone died at a ripe old age, ready for harvest by God.

Grapes on the vine: Christian faith.

Ivy: friendship and affection. Also memory and immortality since the plant is so hardy and difficult to remove.

Lily: innocence and purity. It can also represent the resurrection, as lilies are closely associated with Easter. Because of its connection with the Virgin Mary, they are often carved onto women's graves.

Lily of the valley: innocence, purity, and virginity. Often used on the graves of girls. Rarely used for boys.

Olive branch: peace.

Palm fronds carved on the tympanum of this reverend's grave, possibly showing his occupation in association with palm fronds and Palm Sunday.

Palm: life conquering death and resurrection.

Pansy: humility and remembrance. The name "pansy" comes from the French word *pansée*, meaning "a reflection." Their unique heart-shaped petals also associate this flower with love and affection.

Possible poppies.

Poppy: eternal sleep, peace, and rest. It's said that after her daughter Persephone was taken to the Underworld by Hades, the Greek goddess Demeter ate poppies to fall asleep and forget her grief. Made into opium, poppies were often used as a sleep remedy for adults and even children in the Victorian Era… with overdoses sometimes leading to eternal sleep.

Roses: beauty and virtue. Usually on the grave of a young woman. A broken bud means the girl was younger than 12 years old when she died. A partial bloom means she was a teenager. A full bloom represents a woman who died in the prime of her life. Intertwined rosebuds can mean the death of a mother and infant in childbirth. Appeared as rosettes in the 17th and 18th Centuries and became more lifelike in the Victorian Era.

Tree: protection with their roots embedded in the ground and the canopy offering cover.

Tree stump: often represents a life cut short, and a nest with birds represents the deceased's children. Could be a member of the Woodmen of the World as well as a carpenter, builder, or lumberman.

Weeping willow: the resurrection because a willow tree can be planted from a single branch placed in the ground. It is also melancholy by nature, making it a popular tree planted in rural cemeteries.

Willows (together with urns) were popular symbols in the late 18th and early 19th Centuries.

A zinker (below) from 1884 featuring a sheaf of wheat.

The grave pictured above shows the deceased woman lived 99 years and the sheaf of wheat reflects that.

Wheat: a long life since wheat is harvested after it is ripe and fully matured.

Wreaths: victory over death. Many things in the Victorian Era were connected to their fascination with Ancient Rome. Wreaths on a grave represent when laurels were gifted to winners of races and competitions. In this case, the soul's victory over death as they enter the afterlife.

Other flowers you may see while wandering through the cemetery include:

Acanthus leaves: the difficult or "prickly" journey of life to death due to the flower's spiked leaves. The leaves are often used as decorative foliage on graves to emulate the Ancient Greeks and Romans, as acanthus leaves were found on top of Corinthian columns.

Clover: the Holy Trinity, thanks to its three leaves. It might also denote Irish heritage.

Lotus: spiritual rebirth, reawakening, and resurrection.

Passionflower: is said to represent a belief in Jesus Christ as the flower represents his sacrifice. Its thread-like petals in the center represent the crown of thorns, while the five stamens represent his five wounds, and the 10 outer petals represent his 10 faithful disciples.

Primrose: eternal love, youthfulness, hope, and sadness.

Thistle: with its thorns, it may represent the sacrifice of Christ and his own crown of thorns. Thistles also mean earthly sorrow. It is also the national flower of Scotland, so it may represent someone with Scottish heritage.

Tulip: eternal life and rebirth because they are the only flower that will continue to grow once cut from its bulb.

HANDS

Hands are a common motif you might see while wandering through cemeteries, reminding us of the humanity that comes with death. Not all hands mean the same thing, so keep an eye out for these particular gravestone carvings:

Cohen hand: representative of a priestly blessing. These hands are found on Jewish gravestones, often for someone with the family name Cohen, as the name literally translates to "priest." Said to be directly descended from Aaron, the prophet Moses's brother, these Jewish priests will hold their hands like this while performing an Aaronic blessing. *Star Trek* fans might notice this as the Vulcan salute. Spock actor Leonard Nimoy based it on a priestly blessing he witnessed at an Orthodox synagogue when he was a child.

Sanhedriya Cemetery, Jerusalem.
Photo courtesy of דניאל צבי

Hand holding flowers: may signify when a person's life was cut short. If the flowers are in full bloom, they may have died in the prime of their life. If it is a smaller bud with a broken stem, it could signify that their life was cut short. Hands may also be pointing up, rather than holding the flowers, acting as a reminder that the deceased has gone to Heaven.

Unfortunately, the grave on the left is so worn, we cannot see the age in which she died. However, the grave on the right shows he died at 48 years old in 1887.

Handshake: a reunion, bond, or final farewell. This is perhaps one of the most common motifs you'll find involving hands. Depending on the placement of the hands as well as the details associated with them, you might be able to decipher more about the deceased based on their handshake.

This handshake shows two hands with similar masculine cuffs, possibly signifying a friendship or bond that won't be forgotten.

This grave belongs to a husband and wife. Nestled under a tree, the grave is beautifully preserved, showing the masculine and feminine cuffs, representing their marriage's reunion.

This pair of hands might represent a farewell. The hand on the left is clasped firmly around the stiff fingers on the right, possibly symbolizing a living person saying goodbye to a dead one.

The husband's hand (on the right) is that of a Mason. You can recognize a Mason's handshake by the extension of their pointer finger.

Hand of God: God has come to take the deceased to Heaven. This can be in the form of a hand coming from behind clouds or a curtain, a hand pointed down, or a disembodied hand floating above the scene.

Photo courtesy of Rebecca Czyzewski (@kissing_the_shadows_666)

Hand pointing up: the deceased has gone to Heaven. It encourages those mourning to literally look up.

Other types of hands you might see on graves include:

Hand pointing down: God reaching down to take the deceased to Heaven. It might also represent an unexpected or sudden death that came in the form of an accident.

***Manus Dei*:** the "Hand of God" consisting of two fingers pointing up and two pointing down. Usually used to commemorate a member of the clergy.

ANIMALS AND NATURE

Bats: the Underworld. Since the Middle Ages, bats have been used to symbolize the Devil and evil spirits. You might find these on old Puritan graves from the 17th Century, where dark, morbid imagery was more common.

Photo courtesy of Darren and Jessica Cooke

Beehive: feminine virtues and industriousness. May also represent community as bees work together to build a hive—something they could not accomplish alone. Could also signify a member of the Daughters of Rebekah, the original female branch of the Independent Order of the Oddfellows.

Bird: the soul (particularly if the bird is in flight). Doves are among the most common birds to use due to their association with peace and the Holy Spirit. Eagles are often used to represent an American military background.

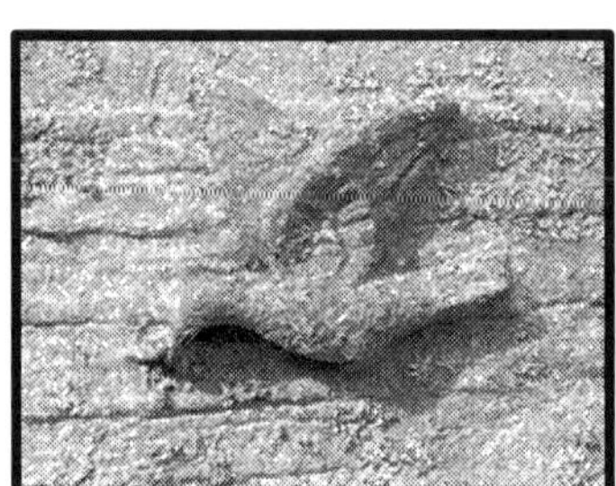

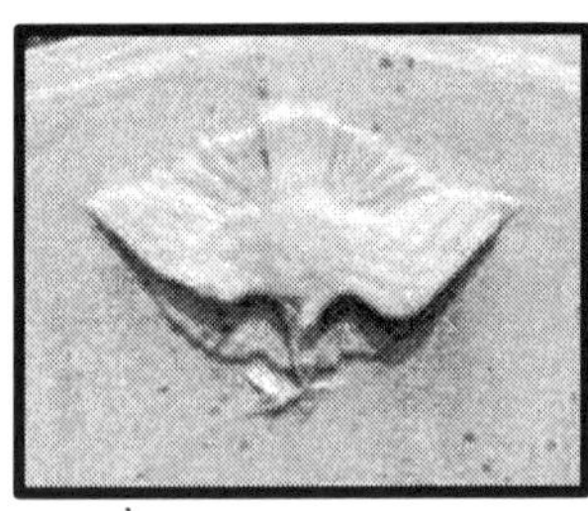

Photo courtesy of Vanessa Stipkovits

A zinker in memory of a veteran of the 10th NY Cavalry during the Civil War. An eagle symbolizes his military service.

Cairns: a prehistoric burial marker constructed of stones of various sizes. Cairns are traditionally found all over the world for various purposes, including burial markers. While the cairn graves found in cemeteries are not built from multiple stones, they are carved from a single piece of marble or granite to recreate the illusion of that ancient tradition.

Lamb: the death of a child. Lambs are associated with purity and innocence, dating back to Ancient Egypt, though most notably in Christianity, with Jesus known as the Lamb of God as well as a shepherd who guides his followers/flock. Still used to symbolize the death of a child even into the 20th Century.

Lambs can be carved into the gravestone or appear as a statue on top.

Mushrooms: life emerging from death and decay just as mushrooms do in the natural world.

Shells: a journey or pilgrimage. Seashells have been a Christian symbol of religious pilgrimages as well as spiritual protection since ancient times.

Stars: divine guidance. A five-pointed star can represent the Star of Bethlehem or the five wounds of Christ, while a six-pointed star may represent the power of God's creation.

Six-pointed stars can be seen in each of the finials of this 18th Century grave.

Sun: the end of earthly life or the dawning of the resurrection represented by a sunrise or sunset.

Other natural elements you may find:

Butterfly: life, death, and resurrection (based on its own three stages of life: the caterpillar, chrysalis, and butterfly).

Dog: loyalty. However, due to the popularity of dogs as pets, they could also represent a specific dog in life.

Fish: faith, as seen with the ancient symbol of Christianity.

Lion: power, courage, and strength. Could represent someone who was seen as a leader.

Owl: wisdom.

Snake: eternity and rebirth. The ability to shed its skin and start anew is significant to one's spiritual journey. If the snake is in a circle, eating its own tail, it is an ouroboros and represents eternity or infinity.

MEMENTO MORI

Grave symbolism of the 17th and early 18th Centuries included frightening imagery of skeletons, skulls, and coffins. These images were the artistic representation of *memento mori*, or a Latin expression that meant "remember you must die." Memento mori was a prevalent theme in artwork, architecture, jewelry, and gravestones during this time. These images were a grave reminder (pun intended) that death was coming, so one must prepare their mind and soul to meet their God. By the late 18th Century and into the Victorian Era of the 19th Century, the macabre imagery used in churchyards was replaced with softer images, making death less frightening and more beautiful.

Crossbones: mortality. Two femurs crossed together, sometimes accompanied by a skull but not always.

Graves from 1739 (top), 1732 (left), and 1683 (right).

Death's head: the most common symbol from 17th Century Puritan cemeteries. Represents death and rebirth when wings are included, making it a "winged Death's head." Eventually turned into cherubs and soul effigies.

Hourglass: time is running out.
Scythe: represents the Grim Reaper.
Skeleton: mortality.
Skull: mortality.

This 1743 grave has it all: an hourglass, crossbones, a skull, a skeleton, and a scythe.

Skull and crossbones and banner that reads MEMENTO MORI in Greyfriars Kirkyard.

Skull and crossbones, coupled with two soul effigies in the finials.

Skull and crossbones: warns of death and acts as a memento mori. A common misconception claims that it symbolizes a wrongful death.

Other reminders of death you might see on graves include:
Bones: mortality.
Coffins: mortality.
Father Time: time is fleeting.
Grim Reaper: death is coming.
Shovels: mortality.
Winged hourglass: the swiftness of time.

FRATERNAL ORDERS

Various fraternal orders are steeped in secrecy, and the graves of their members are no different. However, once you know what to look for, you'll be able to quickly identify something about the individual's life—including what they believed and supported based on the order they may be part of. Many of these orders have their own symbols that can be carved into a gravestone or placed next to the grave as a metal marker.

American Legion: represented by a five-point star and the letters US at the center. This organization encourages peace, patriotism, and goodwill. They work with and for veterans and are determined to post grave markers for every US veteran.

Benevolent Protective Order of Elks (also known as The Elk's Club): represented by an elk and a clock stopped at the eleventh hour. The image of the clock echoes a toast made at any Elks gathering at 11:00 o'clock: "...the golden hour of recollection, the homecoming of those who wander, the mystic roll call of those who will come no more..." Elks are said to believe in charity, justice, brotherly love, and fidelity and work to help their community.

Boy Scouts: represented by the fleur-de-lis since it was once used to signify north on a map, and scouts can show others the way by upholding their duties. The three leaves of the fleur-de-lis are also said to represent a scout's service to others, his duty to God, and obedience to the scout law. Famous Eagle Scouts (the highest rank of a Boy Scout) include Neil Armstrong, Zach Galifianakis, and Steven Spielberg.

Freemasons: most frequently represented by the square and compass with the letter G in the center. The G can represent geometry or God (however, since a belief in a Supreme Being is crucial to be a member, more often than not, it is intended to mean God). The square represents fairness, stability, and a strong foundation, as well as keeping your thoughts and actions true to God and your fellow humans. The compass is used to draw circles, so this is meant to be the spiritual side of life—eternity and infinite possibility. Both the earthly square and the spiritual compass create the perfect balance for a Freemason. Another symbol is the All-Seeing Eye. This represents God, who the Masons see as the architect of the universe. While this image is not nearly as common as the square and compass, you might find an eye carved onto a stone, while the square and compass might be on the grave itself or beside it as a small marker. Freemasonry is the world's oldest and largest fraternal order, having been around for hundreds of years. Traditionally, only men have been permitted to become Freemasons. Some famous Masons include founding fathers George Washington and Benjamin Franklin, Wolfgang Amadeus Mozart, Oscar Wilde, Sir Arthur Conan Doyle, Harry Houdini, Franklin D. Roosevelt, Edwin "Buzz" Aldrin, and Mark Twain.

This grave of a Freemason is denoted by both a grave marker to the left and the symbolism carved into the grave itself. The symbols include the square and compass, stars (to guide the Mason), and the All-Seeing Eye of God.

Fraternal Order of the Eagles: represented by an eagle. Originally established by theatre stagehands, owners, actors, and writers in 1898, they initially offered their members aid with healthcare and funerals. Today, they donate millions of dollars to medical charities.

Independent Order of the Oddfellows: most commonly represented by three chains that sometimes include the letters F, L, and T (friendship, love, and truth). Where other fraternal orders required a specific occupation or social status, this group would accept any odd fellow (hence the name). An extraordinarily charitable group since its inception, they focus on visiting the sick, providing help to the destitute, and ensuring burial is accessible (not just for their members but the public, too). Famous Oddfellows include Charlie Chaplin, P.T. Barnum, Burl Ives, Sir Winston Churchill, and Eleanor Roosevelt.

Photo courtesy of Ann Marie West

Knights of Columbus: represented by a cross pattée and shield. A Catholic fraternity, it provides education, war and disaster relief, and financial aid to members in need. Sometimes referred to as the Catholic Masons.

Knights of Pythias: represented by a skull and crossbones, helmet, swords, and shield, and the initials F, C, and B (friendship, charity, and benevolence). Founded in 1864, today, they help run camps for underprivileged kids and assisted living homes for its elderly members. They also run blood drives and provide scholarships.

Loyal Order of the Moose: represented by a moose head (easy to spot when surrounded by graves decorated with flowers and religious imagery). Established in 1888 (originally as a drinking club), today the focus is on community charities, including Moosehaven—a 70-acre community for retired members—and Mooseheart Child City and School—a 1,000-acre village for needy children and teens. Mooses also donate around $70 million a year to local communities.

Order of the Eastern Star: represented by a five-pointed star (often inverted) with the letters FATAL in each of the star's rays. This comes from the Song of Solomon in the Bible, "Fairest Among Thousands, Altogether Lovely." Founded in 1850 as an all-female alternative to the Freemasons, it was not approved by the Masons until 1873. Today, they donate millions to charities, establish youth organizations, offer student scholarships, and provide housing for their retired members.

Shriners (technically The Imperial Council of the Ancient Arabic Order of the Nobles of the Mystic Shrine): represented by saber swords, inverted moons, and other seemingly Islamic symbols. Established in 1872 by Masons who wanted to have more fun, the Shriners are known for wearing fezzes and driving tiny cars during summer parades. Today, they have founded the Shriners Hospitals for Children, which are free of charge to kids in need. They specialize in helping children with burns and spinal cord injuries, spending $1.6 million on their hospitals *per day.*

Woodmen of the World: represented by incredibly lifelike tree stumps. This fraternity-turned-insurance company was founded in 1882 when a businessman wanted to make life insurance accessible to the common man. They worked under the motto "No Woodmen shall rest in an unmarked grave." Some clues about the deceased's life may rest within the symbolism of the grave. Small logs may represent the number of children the dead man left behind. A nest in one of the branches might also signify a family left behind.

OBJECTS

Anchor: hope as sailors would use anchors to stop and stabilize their ships in rough seas. May also represent a seafaring occupation, such as a sailor, seaman, or someone who served in the Navy.

According to his death records, we know that this man was a sea captain, denoted by the anchor his wife placed on his gravestone.

Angel: God's messengers and our guardians. May be seen mourning or rejoicing. Also used as a way to remind us of God and Heaven that awaits us. Evolved from soul effigies.

Angels can come in different forms from soul effigies (right), cherubs or child-like angels (bottom left), and full-sized (bottom right).

Basket: fertility or a maternal bond.

This tree stump grave is for a man and his wife. Her role as wife and mother may be represented by this basket.

Bench: serves as a place to reminisce and contemplate. The bench might be a stand-alone piece, or a grave itself (these came into popularity during the Victorian Era). If you see a bench in a cemetery, it is acceptable to sit on it as long as it looks strong and sturdy enough. Please make sure you are respectful. Benches often serve as cenotaphs.

Top photo courtesy of Ser Amantio di Nicolao

Book: it could be the Bible (usually labeled) or the book of one's life. If it is closed, it could represent a full and completed life. It could also mean a lifetime of scholarly work or the grave of a teacher.

Chains: what connects a soul to their family. Chains are often found with a broken link, meaning the soul has gone to Heaven. A chain with three links can denote the deceased was a member of the Independent Order of the Oddfellows.

The grave of this 86-year-old woman shows six chain links with several of them broken.

Column: a life suddenly cut short if the column is broken. If it is standing strong and whole, it likely means a full life. These often represent the grave of a husband or young man since columns are supportive, just as a husband or young man would support his family at the time.

Photo courtesy of Jacleen Gianaris

Drapery (also known as Pall): grief and mourning. Often accompanied by an urn but can be gloomily draped over anything.

Drapery or "pall" dates back to ancient times and was a shroud to cover the body. Today, flags often act as palls for veterans, national figures, and royalty. This is where we get the term "pallbearer" from.

Eye: God's eye always watching. Possibly a member of a secret society such as the Freemasons or the Independent Order of the Oddfellows. An eye surrounded by a triangle represents the "All-Seeing Eye."

Half-carved stone: the transition from life to death as something beautiful is emerging from the rough, unpolished stone.

Inverted torch: either a life that has been extinguished or a life that still burns on the other side.

Also known as "The Angel of Death Victorious," the Haserot Angel is a life-sized bronze angel holding an inverted torch, now infamous for seemingly crying black tears. Lakeview Cemetery, Cleveland, OH, Section 9, Lot 14.

IHS: devotion to Jesus Christ, most often denoting the deceased followed the Catholic faith. There are several interpretations of the meaning, though it all comes back to the fact that the individual was a follower of Christianity. These are the first three Greek letters of his name: *Iota* (I), *Eta* (H), and *Sigma* (Σ). IHS can also stand for the Latin expression, *Iesus Hominum Salvator* ("Jesus, savior of mankind"). It could also be the Latin spelling of Jesus: *Ihesus*. It can be seen as both the letters IHS and as a monogram.

You may find the letters IHS on a grave or the IHS monogram that often looks like a $ sign.

Pentacle: possibly the grave of a witch.

Portrait: an attempt to capture the deceased's likeness in life. Originally carved into the gravestone, by the turn of the 20th Century, families could add a porcelain photo to the grave, adding a personal touch.

Due to their fragility, many of these portraits have been lost.

Here lies Interr
the Body of

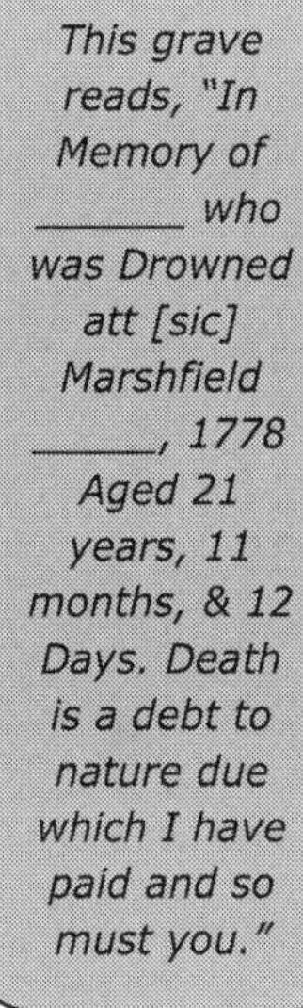

This grave reads, "In Memory of _______ who was Drowned att [sic] Marshfield ______, 1778 Aged 21 years, 11 months, & 12 Days. Death is a debt to nature due which I have paid and so must you."

This minister died in 1787 "in the 86th year of his age and in the 63rd year of his ministry."

Scroll: one's life.

Urn and willow carving (above) and an urn on top of a zinker (left).

Urn: a physical reminder of death. While Victorians did not cremate their dead, the Romans did. Urns are a nod to Ancient Rome and used to show off that someone was familiar with the Classics, cultured, and knowledgeable.

The grave of a woman who died falling from a chaise in 1828 at 25 years old features an urn, willow, and a grieving woman. The woman in the tympanum could be the deceased's mother.

Other items you might find in a cemetery are:

Archway: the passage into the next life.

Bugle: a military career.

Candle: the soul. If the candle is broken, it could be a life that was cut short.

Cannon: a military career.

Clock: the passage of time. Sometimes, the clock can be stopped at the time of death, also known to the Victorians as The Sad Hour.

Crown: the Crown of Righteousness.

Curtains: "the veil" that separates the living from the dead.

Empty chair: often the grave of a young person

Hammer: occupation as a blacksmith.

Harp: worship in Heaven.

Key: spiritual knowledge and access to Heaven.

Lamp: knowledge and a love of learning.

Ship: a seafaring occupation.

Sword: a military career. Two swords crossed could symbolize death in battle.

Wheel: eternity and life's journey. If it is broken, it can symbolize that the journey is over.

PART THREE
CEMETERY WANDERING

SPOT THE GRAVE

We hope you use this book to document your journey through various cemeteries. Whether you wander to familiarize yourself with the inevitability of death, acquaint yourself with your ancestors, or because you're fascinated with history, we hope that this section of the book will provide you with a place to immortalize the deceased you meet and write down notes and any thoughts, emotions, or experiences you might have along the way.

Death comes for all of us, and in the meantime, we must come to terms with the deaths of those we hold most dear. As you explore cemeteries and better understand how our ancestors mourned their dead, we hope you can start to face your own mortality and realize that death is nothing to fear—it is one of the most natural things about life.

The Church of the Holy Rude. Stirling, Scotland.

Break the binding of this book. Take notes. Dog ear your favorite pages. And above all else, don't forget: memento mori.

Where did you find it? ___________________________

Who is buried here? _____________________________

When were they born? ___________________________

When did they die? ______________________________

Is there an epitaph? If so, write it down:

____

____

____

Anything else to note? ___________________________

ACANTHUS LEAVES

The prickly journey of life.

Where did you find it? ______________________________

Who is buried here? _________________________________

When were they born? ______________________________

When did they die? __________________________________

Is there an epitaph? If so, write it down:

____

____

____

Anything else to note? ______________________________

ACORNS AND OAK LEAVES

Humble beginnings. Faith. Strength. Stability.

Left and right photos courtesy of @cemetery_ dryad

Where did you find it? ______________________________

Who is buried here? ________________________________

When were they born? ______________________________

When did they die? _________________________________

Is there an epitaph? If so, write it down:

____

____

____

Anything else to note? ______________________________

ANCHOR

Hope. A seafaring occupation.

Right photo courtesy of Sharni (@urbanhaunts)

Left photo courtesy of Rebecca Czyzewski (@kissing_the_shadows_666)

Where did you find it? ______________________________

Who is buried here? ________________________________

When were they born? ______________________________

When did they die? _________________________________

Is there an epitaph? If so, write it down:

____

____

____

Anything else to note? ______________________________

ANGEL

God's messengers. Our guardians.

Where did you find it? ______________________________

Who is buried here? ________________________________

When were they born? ______________________________

When did they die? __________________________________

Is there an epitaph? If so, write it down:

____

____

____

Anything else to note? ______________________________

ARCHWAY

Passage into the next life.

Arches can be self-standing monuments.
Right photo courtesy of Kari Bergen of Ephemera Obscura

You may find arches carved into gravestones.
Left photo courtesy of Becki Fuller

Where did you find it? ______________________________

Who is buried here? ________________________________

When were they born? ______________________________

When did they die? __________________________________

Is there an epitaph? If so, write it down:

____

____

____

Anything else to note? ______________________________

BASKET

Fertility. Maternal bond.

Where did you find it? ______________________________

Who is buried here? ________________________________

When were they born? ______________________________

When did they die? __________________________________

Is there an epitaph? If so, write it down:

____

____

____

Anything else to note? ______________________________

BAT

The Underworld.

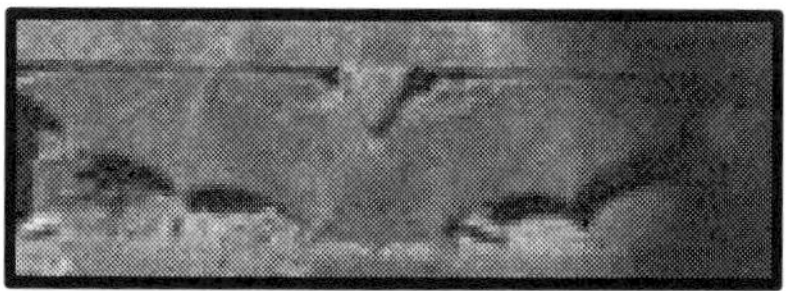

Photo courtesy of Katie Jo Glesing

Photo courtesy of Darren and Jessica Cooke

Where did you find it? ______________________________

Who is buried here? ________________________________

When were they born? ______________________________

When did they die? _________________________________

Is there an epitaph? If so, write it down:

____

____

____

Anything else to note? ______________________________

BEEHIVE

Feminine virtues. Industriousness.

Where did you find it? ______________________________

Who is buried here? ________________________________

When were they born? ______________________________

When did they die? _________________________________

Is there an epitaph? If so, write it down:

____

____

____

Anything else to note? ______________________________

BENCH

Reminiscence. Contemplation.

Right photo courtesy of Tara Feyko

Where did you find it? ____________________________

Who is buried here? ______________________________

When were they born? _____________________________

When did they die? _______________________________

Is there an epitaph? If so, write it down:

____

____

____

Anything else to note? ____________________________

BIRD

The soul. Possibly a veteran.

Left photo courtesy of Jamie Howells and right photo courtesy of Kari Bergen of Ephemera Obscura

Where did you find it? ___________________________

Who is buried here? _____________________________

When were they born? ____________________________

When did they die? ______________________________

Is there an epitaph? If so, write it down:

____

____

____

Anything else to note? ___________________________

BONES

Mortality.

Right photo courtesy of Ryan and Sam L.

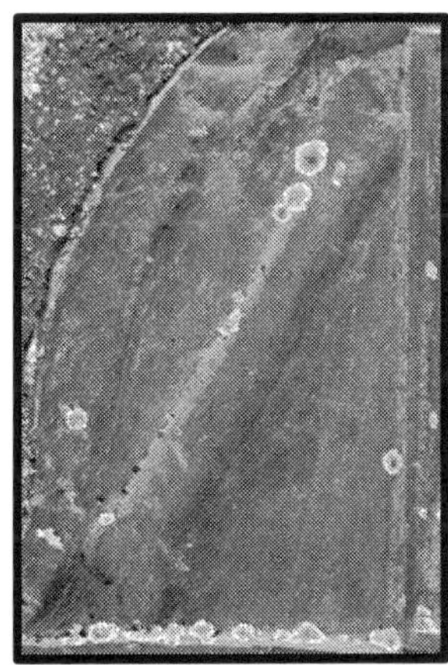

Where did you find it? ______________________________

Who is buried here? ________________________________

When were they born? ______________________________

When did they die? _________________________________

Is there an epitaph? If so, write it down:

____

____

____

Anything else to note? ______________________________

BOOK

The Bible. One's life. A teacher.

Where did you find it? ________________________

Who is buried here? __________________________

When were they born? ________________________

When did they die? ___________________________

Is there an epitaph? If so, write it down:

____

____

____

Anything else to note? ________________________

BUD

The death of a child.

Where did you find it? ______________________________

Who is buried here? ________________________________

When were they born? ______________________________

When did they die? _________________________________

Is there an epitaph? If so, write it down:

____

____

____

Anything else to note? ______________________________

BUTTERFLY

Life. Death. Resurrection.

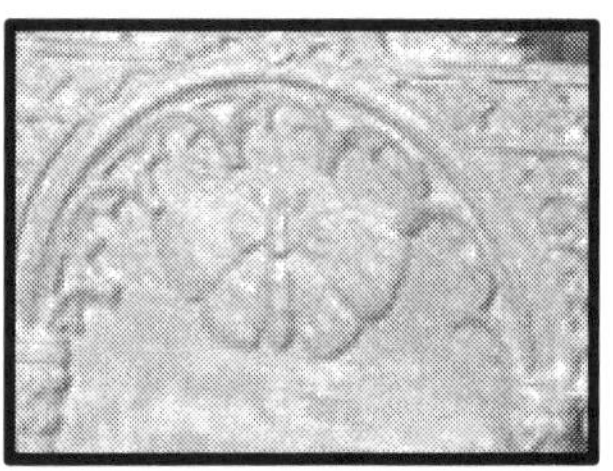

Photo courtesy of Cindy Skawinski

Where did you find it? ___________________________

Who is buried here? _____________________________

When were they born? ___________________________

When did they die? ______________________________

Is there an epitaph? If so, write it down:

____

____

____

Anything else to note? ___________________________

CAIRN

Recreation of prehistoric burial markers.

Where did you find it? ______________________________

Who is buried here? ________________________________

When were they born? ______________________________

When did they die? __________________________________

Is there an epitaph? If so, write it down:

____

____

____

Anything else to note? ______________________________

CALLA LILY

Marriage.

Bottom photo courtesy of Jay Rhoads (@m_t_graves)

Where did you find it? ______________________________

Who is buried here? ________________________________

When were they born? ______________________________

When did they die? _________________________________

Is there an epitaph? If so, write it down:

____

____

____

Anything else to note? ______________________________

CANDLE

The soul.

Photo courtesy of Mindi Ridgeway

Photo courtesy of Becki Fuller

Where did you find it? ______________________________

Who is buried here? ________________________________

When were they born? ______________________________

When did they die? _________________________________

Is there an epitaph? If so, write it down:

____

____

____

Anything else to note? ______________________________

CANNON

A military career.

Where did you find it? ___________________________

Who is buried here? ______________________________

When were they born? ____________________________

When did they die? _______________________________

Is there an epitaph? If so, write it down:

____

____

____

Anything else to note? ___________________________

CHAINS

Connects a soul to their family.

Where did you find it? ______________________________

Who is buried here? ________________________________

When were they born? ______________________________

When did they die? __________________________________

Is there an epitaph? If so, write it down:

____

____

____

Anything else to note? ______________________________

CLOCK

Passage of time. The Sad Hour.

Right photo courtesy of Danielle "Verona Black" Gonzalez

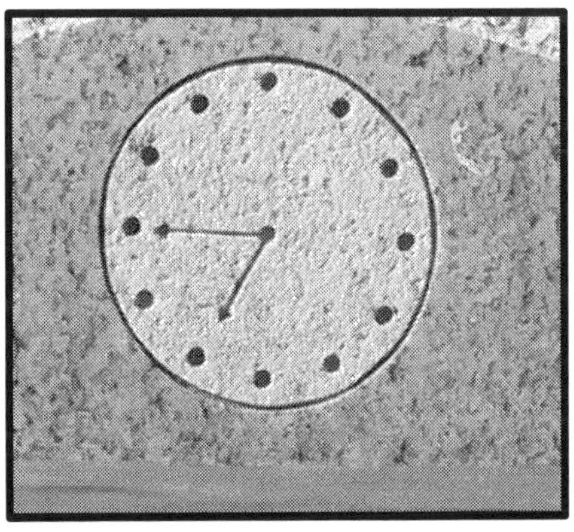

Left photo courtesy of @cemetery_dryad

Where did you find it? ______________________________

Who is buried here? _________________________________

When were they born? ______________________________

When did they die? __________________________________

Is there an epitaph? If so, write it down:

____

____

____

Anything else to note? ______________________________

CLOVER

The Holy Trinity. Irish heritage.

Where did you find it? ______________________________

Who is buried here? ________________________________

When were they born? ______________________________

When did they die? _________________________________

Is there an epitaph? If so, write it down:

____

____

____

Anything else to note? ______________________________

COFFIN

Mortality. Memento mori.

Photos courtesy of Leah Griffiths

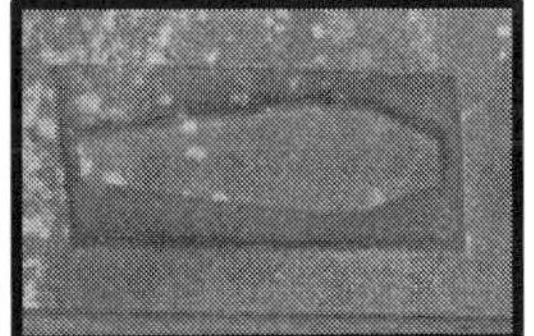

Where did you find it? ______________________________

Who is buried here? ________________________________

When were they born? ______________________________

When did they die? _________________________________

Is there an epitaph? If so, write it down:

____

____

____

Anything else to note? ______________________________

COHEN HAND

Priestly blessing.

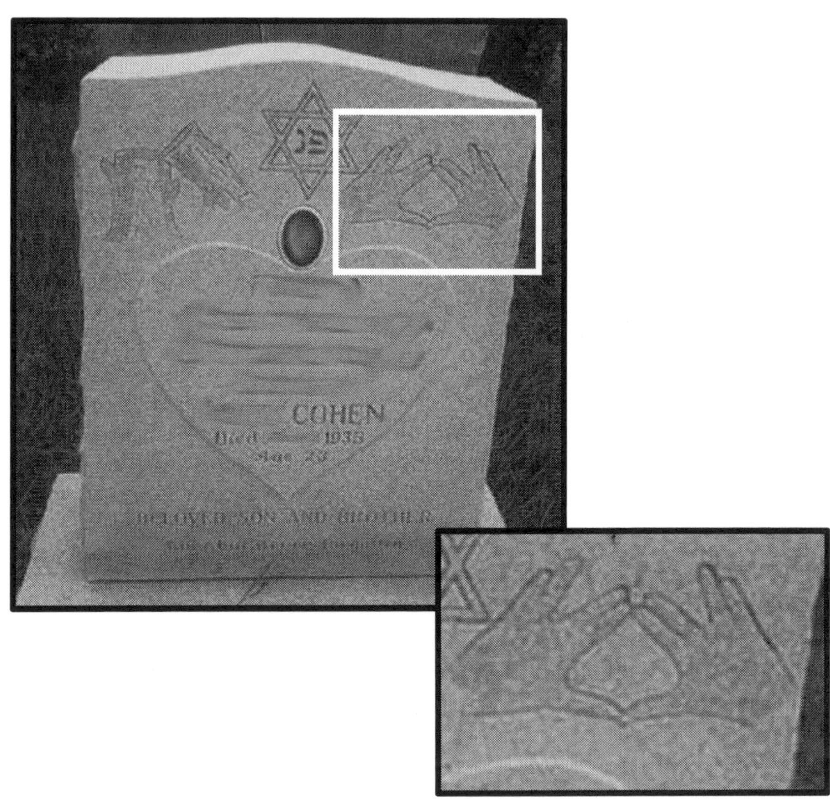

Photo courtesy of @cemetery_dryad

Where did you find it? ______________________________

Who is buried here? ________________________________

When were they born? ______________________________

When did they die? _________________________________

Is there an epitaph? If so, write it down:

____

____

____

Anything else to note? ______________________________

COLUMN

A life.

Photo courtesy of @cemetery_dryad

Where did you find it? ______________________________

Who is buried here? _________________________________

When were they born? ______________________________

When did they die? _________________________________

Is there an epitaph? If so, write it down:

____

____

____

Anything else to note? ______________________________

CORN

Long life. A farming occupation.

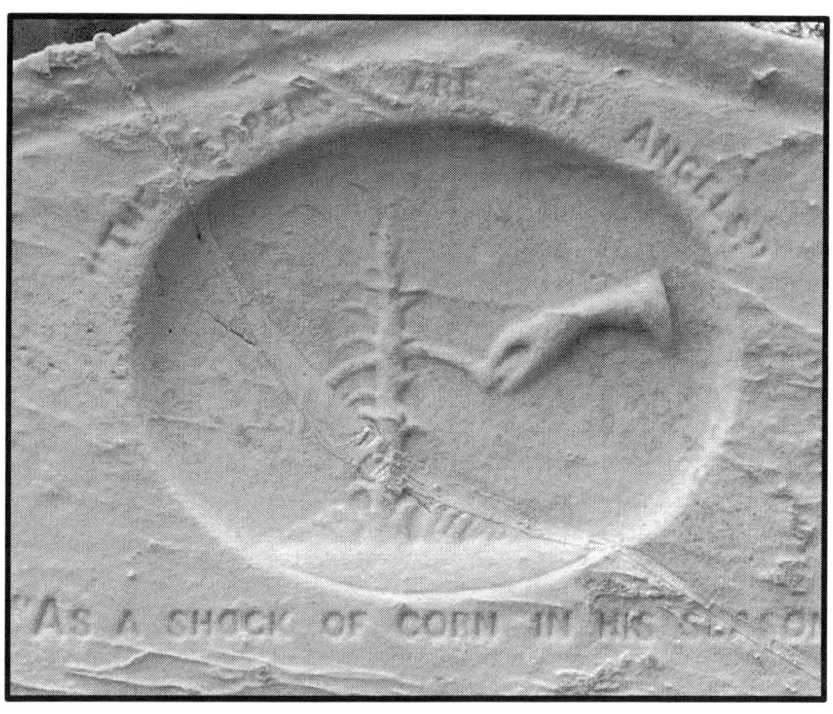

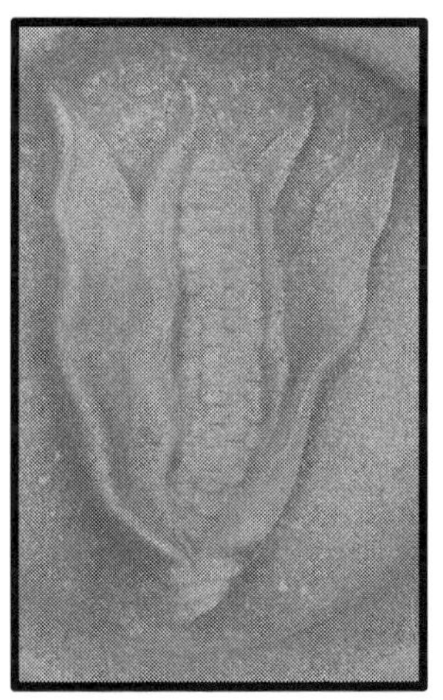

Left photo courtesy of @cemetery_dryad

Where did you find it? ______________________________

Who is buried here? ________________________________

When were they born? ______________________________

When did they die? _________________________________

Is there an epitaph? If so, write it down:

____

____

____

Anything else to note? ______________________________

CROSSBONES

Mortality. Memento mori.

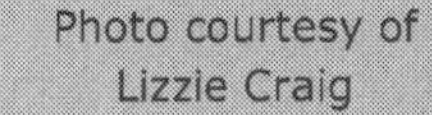

Photo courtesy of Lizzie Craig

Photo courtesy of Ryan and Sam L.

Where did you find it? ______________________________

Who is buried here? ________________________________

When were they born? _____________________________

When did they die? _________________________________

Is there an epitaph? If so, write it down:

____

____

____

Anything else to note? ______________________________

CROWN

The Crown of Righteousness.

Photo courtesy of Jasmine Kuzela

Photo courtesy of @to_the_graveyard_anais

Where did you find it? ______________________________

Who is buried here? ________________________________

When were they born? ______________________________

When did they die? _________________________________

Is there an epitaph? If so, write it down:

____

____

____

Anything else to note? ______________________________

CURTAINS

The veil that separates the living and the dead.

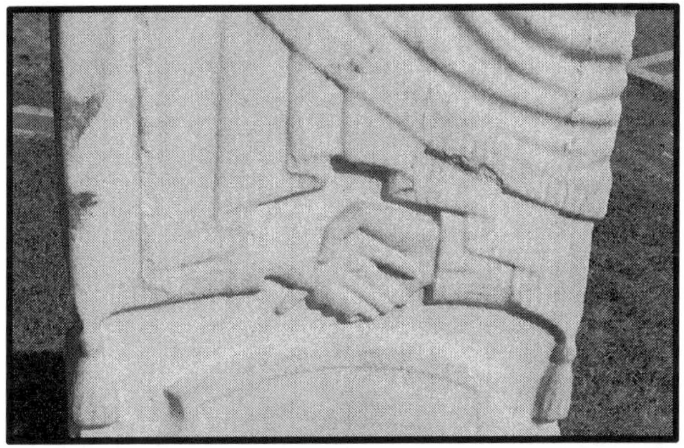

Also note the extended pointer finger, denoting a Mason.
Photo courtesy of @cemetery_dryad

Where did you find it? ______________________________

Who is buried here? ________________________________

When were they born? ______________________________

When did they die? __________________________________

Is there an epitaph? If so, write it down:

____

____

____

Anything else to note? ______________________________

DAISY

The death of a child.

Photo courtesy of
@to_the_graveyard_anais

A daisy found on a family's zinker. The daisy and unopened bud could signify the death of a child.

Where did you find it? ______________________________

Who is buried here? ________________________________

When were they born? ______________________________

When did they die? _________________________________

Is there an epitaph? If so, write it down:

____

____

____

Anything else to note? ______________________________

DAFFODIL

The flower of the Underworld.

Where did you find it? ______________________________

Who is buried here? ________________________________

When were they born? _______________________________

When did they die? _________________________________

Is there an epitaph? If so, write it down:

____

____

____

Anything else to note? ______________________________

DEATH'S HEAD

Death. Rebirth.

Where did you find it? ______________________________

Who is buried here? ________________________________

When were they born? ______________________________

When did they die? __________________________________

Is there an epitaph? If so, write it down:

____

____

____

Anything else to note? ______________________________

DOG

Loyalty.

Where did you find it? ______________________________

Who is buried here? ________________________________

When were they born? ______________________________

When did they die? __________________________________

Is there an epitaph? If so, write it down:

____

____

____

Anything else to note? ______________________________

DRAPERY / PALL

Grief. Mourning.

Where did you find it? ______________________________

Who is buried here? ________________________________

When were they born? ______________________________

When did they die? _________________________________

Is there an epitaph? If so, write it down:

____

____

____

Anything else to note? ______________________________

EMPTY CHAIR

The death of a child.

A grave for a young boy with an epitaph that reads, In Grandma's Care.
Photo courtesy of Amanda Montanari

Where did you find it? ______________________________

Who is buried here? ________________________________

When were they born? ______________________________

When did they die? _________________________________

Is there an epitaph? If so, write it down:

____

____

____

Anything else to note? ______________________________

EYE

God's eye watching.

Left image courtesy of @cemetery_dryad and right photo courtesy of Cindy Skawinski

Where did you find it? ______________________________

Who is buried here? ________________________________

When were they born? ______________________________

When did they die? __________________________________

Is there an epitaph? If so, write it down:

____

____

____

Anything else to note? ______________________________

FATHER TIME

Time is fleeting.

Father Time with his hourglass (right) and the Grim Reaper (left) snuffing out the candle of the young man's life on this 1678 grave.
Photo courtesy of Smell of Fear Candle Co.

Where did you find it? ______________________________

Who is buried here? ________________________________

When were they born? ______________________________

When did they die? __________________________________

Is there an epitaph? If so, write it down:

____

____

____

Anything else to note? ______________________________

FERN

Sincerity. Humility. Solitude.

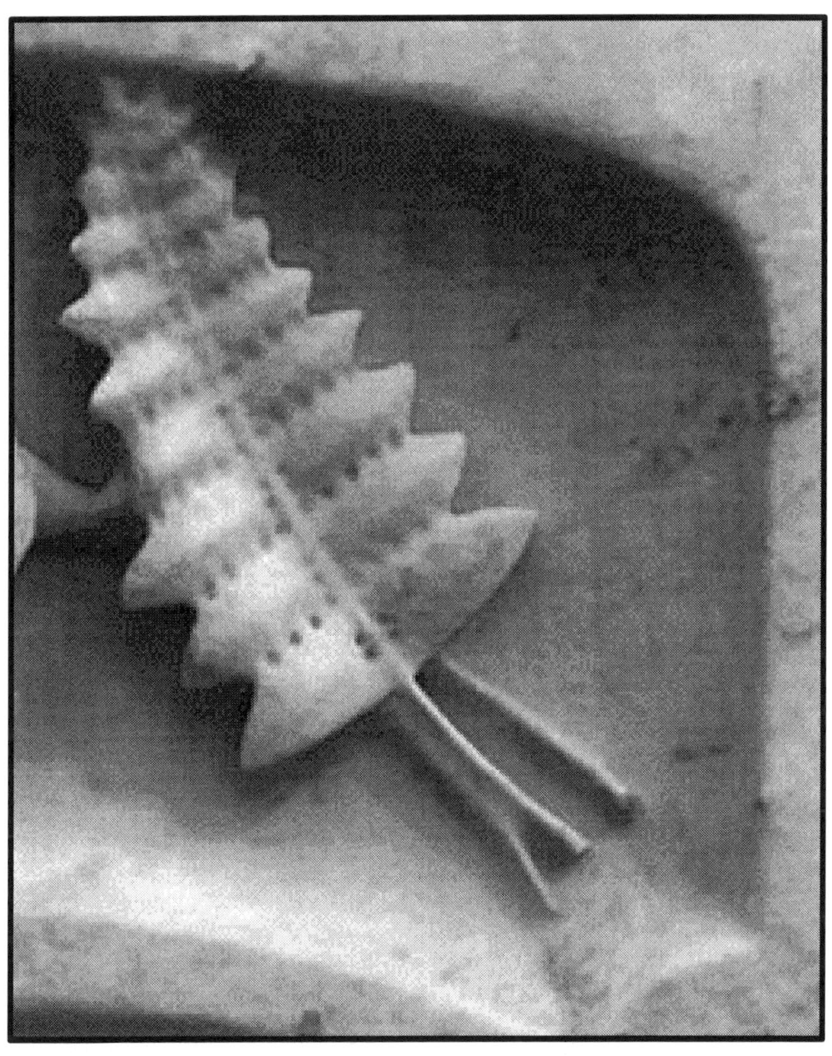

Where did you find it? ___________________________

Who is buried here? ____________________________

When were they born? ___________________________

When did they die? _____________________________

Is there an epitaph? If so, write it down:

____

____

____

Anything else to note? __________________________

FISH

Faith.

Where did you find it? ____________________________

Who is buried here? ______________________________

When were they born? ____________________________

When did they die? _______________________________

Is there an epitaph? If so, write it down:

____

____

____

Anything else to note? ____________________________

FORGET-ME-NOT

Remembrance. Eternal love. Faithfulness.

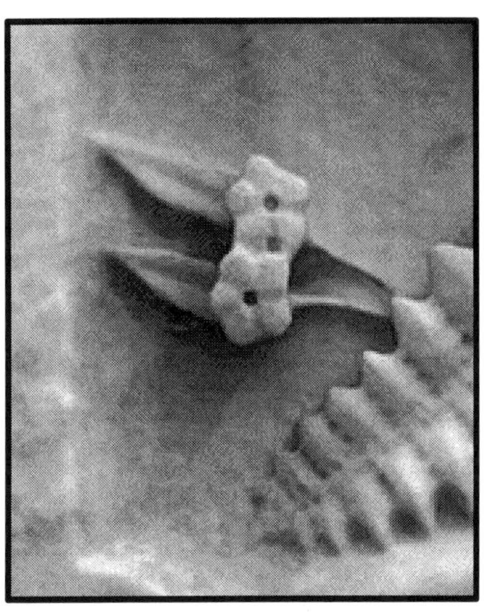

Where did you find it? ______________________________

Who is buried here? ________________________________

When were they born? ______________________________

When did they die? _________________________________

Is there an epitaph? If so, write it down:

____

____

____

Anything else to note? ______________________________

GRAPES

Long life. Christian faith.

Where did you find it? ______________________________

Who is buried here? ________________________________

When were they born? ______________________________

When did they die? _________________________________

Is there an epitaph? If so, write it down:

____

____

____

Anything else to note? ______________________________

GRIM REAPER

Death is coming.

Photo courtesy of Ryan and Sam L.

Where did you find it? ______________________________

Who is buried here? ________________________________

When were they born? ______________________________

When did they die? _________________________________

Is there an epitaph? If so, write it down:

____

____

____

Anything else to note? ______________________________

HALF-CARVED STONE

The transition from life to death.

Where did you find it? ___________________________

Who is buried here? _____________________________

When were they born? ___________________________

When did they die? _______________________________

Is there an epitaph? If so, write it down:

____

____

____

Anything else to note? ___________________________

HAMMER

A blacksmith occupation.

Photo courtesy of Paige Dalton

Where did you find it? ______________________________

Who is buried here? ________________________________

When were they born? ______________________________

When did they die? _________________________________

Is there an epitaph? If so, write it down:

____

____

____

Anything else to note? ______________________________

HAND HOLDING FLOWERS

A life cut short.

Photo courtesy of @cemetery_dryad

Where did you find it? ____________________________

Who is buried here? ______________________________

When were they born? ____________________________

When did they die? _______________________________

Is there an epitaph? If so, write it down:

____

____

____

Anything else to note? ___________________________

HAND OF GOD

God taking the deceased to Heaven.

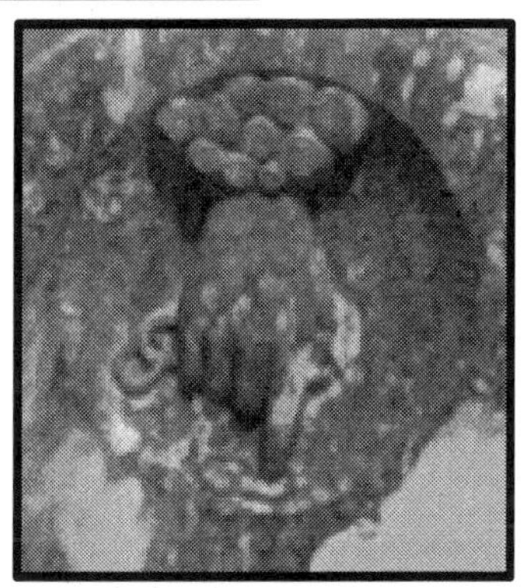

The top image shows a hand coming out of the clouds while holding a flower to add a bit of femininity to the wife's grave. The bottom photos show a hand coming from the clouds while holding a broken chain. Top photo courtesy of Leah Griffiths, bottom left photo courtesy of Becki Fuller, and bottom right photo courtesy of Rebecca Czyzewski (@kissing_the_shadows_666)

Where did you find it? ______________________________

Who is buried here? ________________________________

When were they born? ______________________________

When did they die? _________________________________

Is there an epitaph? If so, write it down:

____

____

____

Anything else to note? ______________________________

HAND POINTING DOWN

God coming to claim a life. An unexpected death.

Photo courtesy of @cemetery_dryad

Where did you find it? ____________________________

Who is buried here? ________________________________

When were they born? ______________________________

When did they die? _________________________________

Is there an epitaph? If so, write it down:

____

____

____

Anything else to note? ______________________________

HAND POINTING UP

The deceased has gone to Heaven.

Where did you find it? ______________________________

Who is buried here? ________________________________

When were they born? ______________________________

When did they die? _________________________________

Is there an epitaph? If so, write it down:

____

____

____

Anything else to note? ______________________________

HANDSHAKE

Farewell. Reunion. Friendship.

Where did you find it? ______________________________

Who is buried here? ________________________________

When were they born? ______________________________

When did they die? _________________________________

Is there an epitaph? If so, write it down:

____

____

____

Anything else to note? ______________________________

HARP

Worship in Heaven.

Where did you find it? ______________________________

Who is buried here? ________________________________

When were they born? ______________________________

When did they die? _________________________________

Is there an epitaph? If so, write it down:

____

____

____

Anything else to note? ______________________________

HOURGLASS

Time is running out.

Photo courtesy of Danielle "Verona Black" Gonzalez

Bottom right photo in honor of an innocent victim of the Salem Witch Trials.
Right photo courtesy of Tracy Rose

Where did you find it? ______________________________

Who is buried here? _________________________________

When were they born? ______________________________

When did they die? __________________________________

Is there an epitaph? If so, write it down:

____

____

____

Anything else to note? ______________________________

IHS

Faith in Jesus Christ.

Where did you find it? ______________________________

Who is buried here? ________________________________

When were they born? ______________________________

When did they die? _________________________________

Is there an epitaph? If so, write it down:

____

____

____

Anything else to note? ______________________________

INVERTED TORCH

A life snuffed out. A life that still burns on the other side.

Photo courtesy of Stephanie Molner

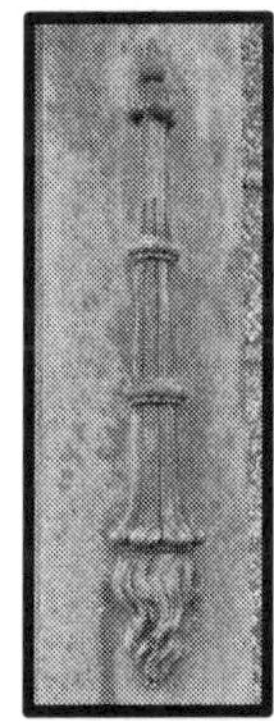

Outer photos courtesy of Danielle "Verona Black" Gonzalez and inner photo courtesy of Elizabeth Martin

Where did you find it? ______________________________

Who is buried here? ________________________________

When were they born? ______________________________

When did they die? _________________________________

Is there an epitaph? If so, write it down:

____

____

____

Anything else to note? ______________________________

IVY

Friendship. Affection. Immortality.

Photo courtesy of Caroline Bennett

Where did you find it? ______________________________

Who is buried here? ________________________________

When were they born? ______________________________

When did they die? _________________________________

Is there an epitaph? If so, write it down:

____

____

____

Anything else to note? ______________________________

LAMB

The death of a child.

Where did you find it? ______________________________

Who is buried here? ________________________________

When were they born? ______________________________

When did they die? __________________________________

Is there an epitaph? If so, write it down:

____

____

____

Anything else to note? ______________________________

LAMP

Knowledge. Love of learning.

Where did you find it? ______________________________

Who is buried here? ________________________________

When were they born? ______________________________

When did they die? ________________________________

Is there an epitaph? If so, write it down:

____

____

____

Anything else to note? _____________________________

LILY

Innocence. Purity.

Where did you find it? ______________________________

Who is buried here? ________________________________

When were they born? ______________________________

When did they die? __________________________________

Is there an epitaph? If so, write it down:

____

____

____

Anything else to note? ______________________________

LILY OF THE VALLEY

Innocence. Purity. Virginity.

A young girl's grave.
Above photo courtesy of Tracy Rose

Photo below found on a family's zinker.
Below photo courtesy of Michele Baumann

Where did you find it? ______________________________

Who is buried here? ________________________________

When were they born? ______________________________

When did they die? _________________________________

Is there an epitaph? If so, write it down:

____

____

____

Anything else to note? ______________________________

LION

Power. Courage. Strength.

Photo courtesy of Emma K. Isnor

Photo courtesy of Ryan and Shayna Muckerheide, the three-times great-granddaughter of the interred.

Where did you find it? ________________________

Who is buried here? __________________________

When were they born? ________________________

When did they die? ___________________________

Is there an epitaph? If so, write it down:

____

____

____

Anything else to note? ________________________

MARRIAGE HANDSHAKE

A matrimonial reunion.

Photo courtesy of @cemetery_dryad

Where did you find it? ______________________________

Who is buried here? ________________________________

When were they born? ______________________________

When did they die? _________________________________

Is there an epitaph? If so, write it down:

____

____

____

Anything else to note? ______________________________

MASON HANDSHAKE.

Reunion or farewell with a Mason.

Right photo courtesy of Kari Bergen of Ephemera Obscura

Where did you find it? ______________________________

Who is buried here? ________________________________

When were they born? ______________________________

When did they die? _________________________________

Is there an epitaph? If so, write it down:

____

____

____

Anything else to note? ______________________________

MUSHROOMS

Growth from decay.

Where did you find it? ______________________________

Who is buried here? ________________________________

When were they born? ______________________________

When did they die? _________________________________

Is there an epitaph? If so, write it down:

____

____

____

Anything else to note? ______________________________

ODDFELLOW CHAIN

Member of the Independent Order of the Oddfellows.

Where did you find it? ______________________________

Who is buried here? ________________________________

When were they born? ______________________________

When did they die? _________________________________

Is there an epitaph? If so, write it down:

____

____

____

Anything else to note? ______________________________

OLIVE BRANCH

Peace.

Where did you find it? ______________________________

Who is buried here? ________________________________

When were they born? _______________________________

When did they die? __________________________________

Is there an epitaph? If so, write it down:

____

____

____

Anything else to note? ______________________________

OWL

Wisdom.

Photo courtesy of Katie Jo Glesing

Where did you find it? ______________________________

Who is buried here? ________________________________

When were they born? ______________________________

When did they die? _________________________________

Is there an epitaph? If so, write it down:

____

____

____

Anything else to note? ______________________________

PALM

Life conquering death. Resurrection.

Where did you find it? ______________________________

Who is buried here? ________________________________

When were they born? ______________________________

When did they die? _________________________________

Is there an epitaph? If so, write it down:

____

____

____

Anything else to note? ______________________________

PANSY

Humility. Remembrance.

Where did you find it? ______________________________

Who is buried here? ________________________________

When were they born? ______________________________

When did they die? _________________________________

Is there an epitaph? If so, write it down:

____

____

____

Anything else to note? ______________________________

PASSION FLOWER

Belief in Jesus Christ and His sacrifice.

Left photo courtesy of @to_the_graveyard_anais and right photo courtesy of Diane E. Chambers

Where did you find it? ______________________________

Who is buried here? ________________________________

When were they born? ______________________________

When did they die? _________________________________

Is there an epitaph? If so, write it down:

____

____

____

Anything else to note? _____________________________

PENTACLE

A witch's grave.

Where did you find it? ______________________________

Who is buried here? ________________________________

When were they born? ______________________________

When did they die? _________________________________

Is there an epitaph? If so, write it down:

____

____

____

Anything else to note? ______________________________

POPPY

Eternal rest.

Where did you find it? ______________________________

Who is buried here? ________________________________

When were they born? ______________________________

When did they die? __________________________________

Is there an epitaph? If so, write it down:

____

____

____

Anything else to note? ______________________________

PORTRAIT

The likeness of someone in life.

Where did you find it? ______________________________

Who is buried here? ________________________________

When were they born? _______________________________

When did they die? _________________________________

Is there an epitaph? If so, write it down:

____

____

____

Anything else to note? ______________________________

ROSE

Beauty. Virtue.

Where did you find it? ______________________________

Who is buried here? ________________________________

When were they born? ______________________________

When did they die? _________________________________

Is there an epitaph? If so, write it down:

____

____

____

Anything else to note? ______________________________

SCROLL

One's life.

Where did you find it? ______________________________

Who is buried here? _________________________________

When were they born? ______________________________

When did they die? __________________________________

Is there an epitaph? If so, write it down:

____

____

____

Anything else to note? ______________________________

SCYTHE

The Grim Reaper.

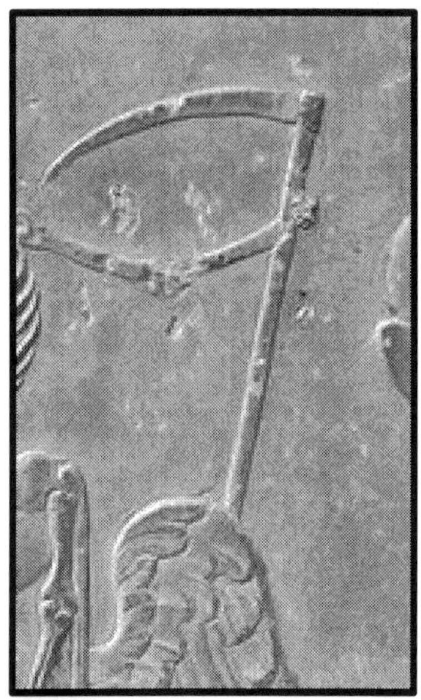

A scythe behind an hourglass on a zinker.
Photo courtesy of Haiden Nelson

Where did you find it? ____________________________

Who is buried here? ______________________________

When were they born? ____________________________

When did they die? _______________________________

Is there an epitaph? If so, write it down:

____

____

____

Anything else to note? ____________________________

SHELL

A pilgrimage.

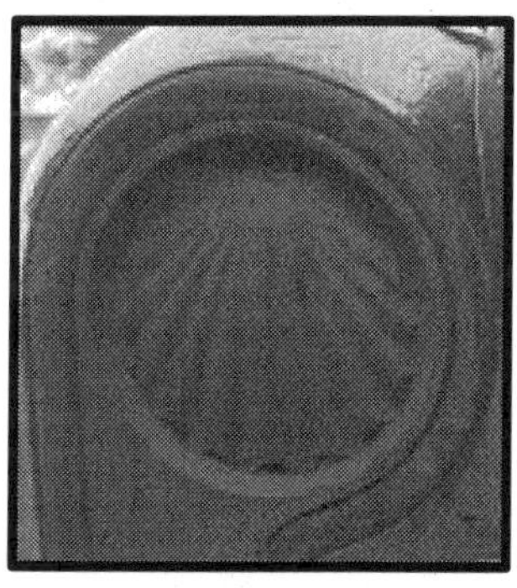

Where did you find it? ______________________________

Who is buried here? ________________________________

When were they born? ______________________________

When did they die? __________________________________

Is there an epitaph? If so, write it down:

____

____

____

Anything else to note? ______________________________

SHIP

A seafaring occupation.

Left photo courtesy of Ryan and Sam L. and right photo courtesy of Ivy Brandine

Where did you find it? ______________________________

Who is buried here? ________________________________

When were they born? ______________________________

When did they die? _________________________________

Is there an epitaph? If so, write it down:

____

____

____

Anything else to note? ______________________________

SHOVEL

Mortality. Memento mori.

Photo courtesy of Caroline Bennett

Left photos courtesy of Lizzie Craig and right photo courtesy of Cedric Justice

Where did you find it? ____________________________

Who is buried here? ______________________________

When were they born? ____________________________

When did they die? _______________________________

Is there an epitaph? If so, write it down:

____

____

____

Anything else to note? ____________________________

SKELETON

Mortality. Memento mori.

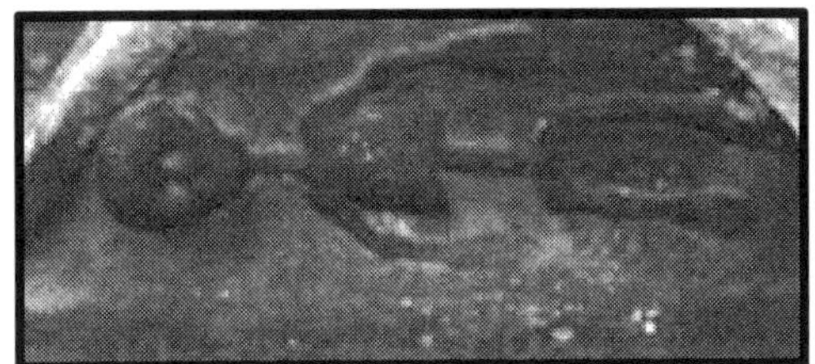

Where did you find it? ____________________

Who is buried here? ____________________

When were they born? ____________________

When did they die? ____________________

Is there an epitaph? If so, write it down:

____

____

____

Anything else to note? ____________________

SKULL

Mortality. Memento mori.

Where did you find it? ______________________________

Who is buried here? ________________________________

When were they born? ______________________________

When did they die? _________________________________

Is there an epitaph? If so, write it down:

____

____

____

Anything else to note? ______________________________

SKULL AND CROSSBONES

Mortality. Memento mori.

Where did you find it? ______________________________

Who is buried here? ________________________________

When were they born? ______________________________

When did they die? _________________________________

Is there an epitaph? If so, write it down:

____

____

____

Anything else to note? ______________________________

SNAKE

Eternity. Rebirth.

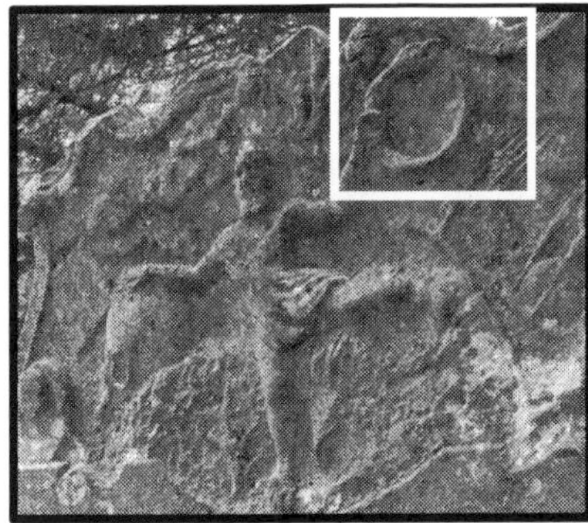

The snake eating its tail is an ouroboros. Photo courtesy of @to_the_graveyard_anais

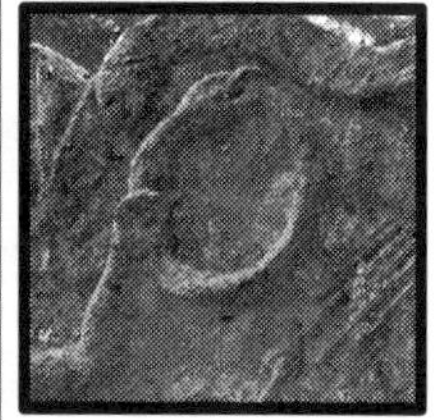

Perhaps the most famous grave in all of New England. The skeleton with a laurel symbolizes victory over death. The sun and the moon can denote the heavenly bodies. The angels in the top corners and the bats in the bottom corners show good triumphing over evil. The snake in a perfect circle represents eternity.
Photo courtesy of Susan Jacobucci

Where did you find it? ______________________________

Who is buried here? ________________________________

When were they born? ______________________________

When did they die? ________________________________

Is there an epitaph? If so, write it down:

____

____

____

Anything else to note? ______________________________

SOUL EFFIGY

The soul.

Where did you find it? ______________________________

Who is buried here? ________________________________

When were they born? _______________________________

When did they die? __________________________________

Is there an epitaph? If so, write it down:

____

____

____

Anything else to note? ______________________________

SQUARE AND COMPASS

A member of the Freemasons.

Where did you find it? ______________________________

Who is buried here? ________________________________

When were they born? ______________________________

When did they die? _________________________________

Is there an epitaph? If so, write it down:

____

____

____

Anything else to note? ______________________________

STAR

Divine guidance.

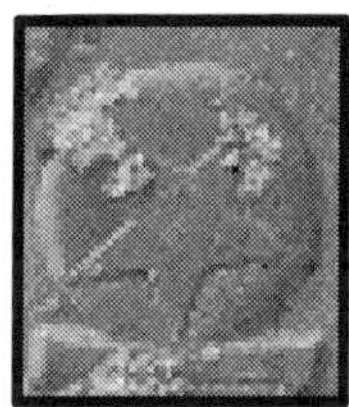

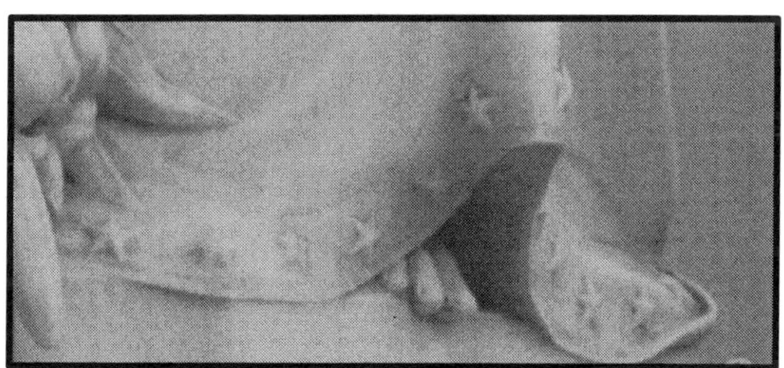

Photo courtesy of @thedyerghoulhouse

Where did you find it? ______________________________

Who is buried here? _________________________________

When were they born? _______________________________

When did they die? __________________________________

Is there an epitaph? If so, write it down:

____

____

____

Anything else to note? ______________________________

SUN

The end of earthly life. Dawning of the resurrection.

Bottom photo courtesy of Vanessa Stipkovits

Where did you find it? ______________________________

Who is buried here? ________________________________

When were they born? ______________________________

When did they die? _________________________________

Is there an epitaph? If so, write it down:

____

____

____

Anything else to note? ______________________________

SWORD

A military career.

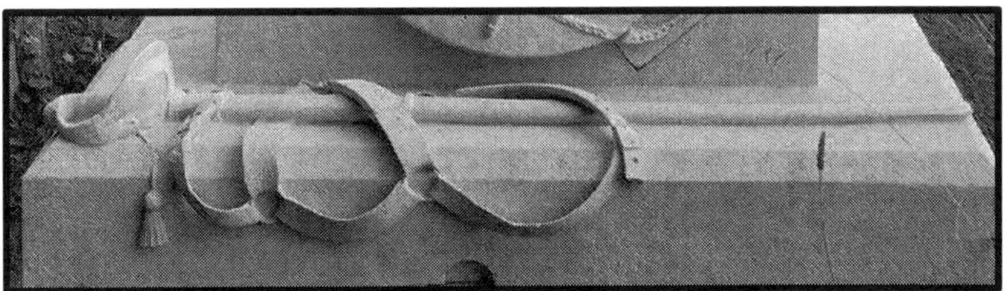

Photo courtesy of @to_the_graveyard_anais

Photo courtesy of Mindi Ridgeway

Where did you find it? ______________________________

Who is buried here? ________________________________

When were they born? ______________________________

When did they die? _________________________________

Is there an epitaph? If so, write it down:

____

____

____

Anything else to note? ______________________________

THISTLE

The sacrifice of Christ. Scottish heritage.

Photo courtesy of Cindy Skawinski

Where did you find it? ______________________________

Who is buried here? ________________________________

When were they born? ______________________________

When did they die? __________________________________

Is there an epitaph? If so, write it down:

____

____

____

Anything else to note? ______________________________

TREE

Protection.

Where did you find it? ______________________________

Who is buried here? ________________________________

When were they born? ______________________________

When did they die? __________________________________

Is there an epitaph? If so, write it down:

____

____

____

Anything else to note? ______________________________

TREE STUMP

Life cut short. Member of the Woodmen of the World.

Where did you find it? ______________________________

Who is buried here? ________________________________

When were they born? ______________________________

When did they die? __________________________________

Is there an epitaph? If so, write it down:

____

____

____

Anything else to note? ______________________________

TULIP

Eternal life. Rebirth.

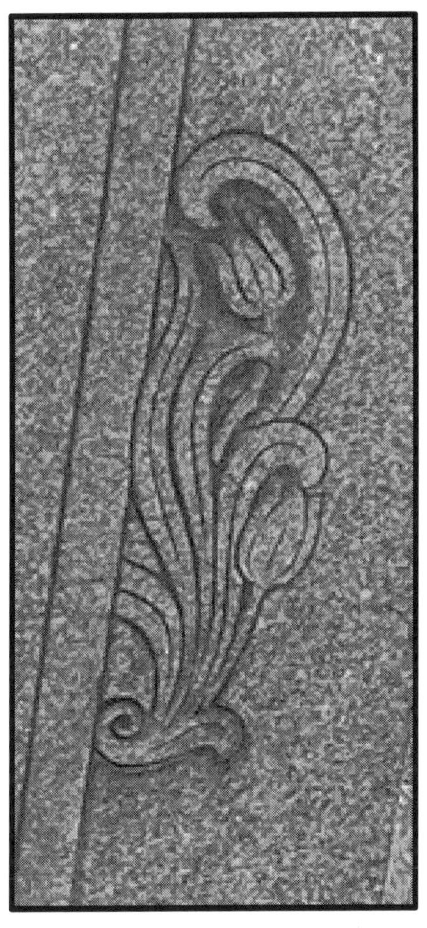

Where did you find it? ______________________________

Who is buried here? ________________________________

When were they born? ______________________________

When did they die? _________________________________

Is there an epitaph? If so, write it down:

____

____

____

Anything else to note? ______________________________

URN

The physical reminder of death.

Where did you find it? ________________________

Who is buried here? ________________________

When were they born? ________________________

When did they die? ________________________

Is there an epitaph? If so, write it down:

____

____

____

Anything else to note? ________________________

WEEPING WILLOW

Melancholy. The resurrection.

Where did you find it? ______________________________

Who is buried here? _________________________________

When were they born? ______________________________

When did they die? _________________________________

Is there an epitaph? If so, write it down:

____

____

____

Anything else to note? ______________________________

WHEAT

A long life.

Where did you find it? ______________________________

Who is buried here? ________________________________

When were they born? ______________________________

When did they die? ___________________________________

Is there an epitaph? If so, write it down:

____

____

____

Anything else to note? ______________________________

WINGED HOURGLASS

The swiftness of time.

Above photo courtesy of Vera Ahrweiler (@tombstone.tourism)
Left photo below courtesy of Leanna Renee Hieber and right photo below courtesy of @thedyerghoulhouse

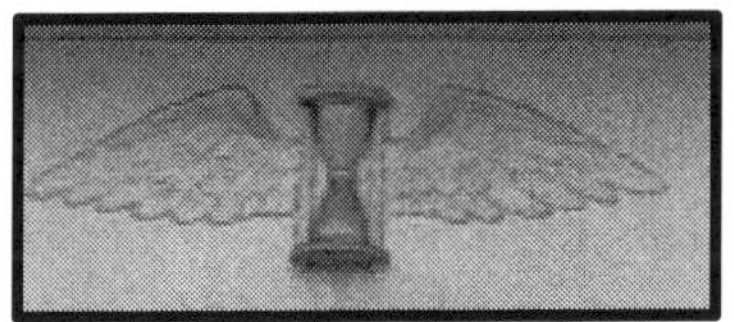

Where did you find it? ______________________________

Who is buried here? ________________________________

When were they born? ______________________________

When did they die? _________________________________

Is there an epitaph? If so, write it down:

____

____

____

Anything else to note? ______________________________

WREATH

Victory over death.

COME LITTLE CHILDREN

Today, the death of a young person, regardless of their age, is a tragedy—the loss is profound and seen as unnatural. However, until fairly recently (within the last century, to be precise), losing a child (and possibly even multiple children) was a common occurrence. In many instances, couples would begin to have as many children as possible—sometimes, Victorian women would be constantly pregnant from marriage to menopause—knowing full well that not all of their sons and daughters would make it through childhood. Not only were families prepared to endure a child's death, but they expected it.

By the mid-19th Century, child mortality rates (as well as maternal mortality rates in childbirth) were extremely high. It has been estimated that 31,000 women died in childbirth in England and Wales alone in the 1850s. Wealth could not protect you against losing a child, and a variety of causes could lead to a child's death, such as poor

sanitation and nutrition, bad milk, lead-painted toys, and arsenic in the wallpaper.

Infant mortality rates ranged considerably between urban and rural environments. Larger cities and industrial towns were overcrowded and unsanitary, often with sewage running through the streets and contaminated drinking water that could easily spread diseases to newborns and infants. With the sudden rise in industrialization, we also see an increase in urbanization—individuals and families moving from small towns and villages to larger cities, hoping to find work. As the cities grew more crowded, infant mortality rates skyrocketed, with some of the highest percentages seen in large cities such as London and New York.

It's believed that for every 1,000 successful births, 46% would not live to see their fifth birthday.

Many cemeteries are the eternal homes of small children, with their graves often marked with lambs.

Use this section of the book to stop and get to know the children buried beneath the lambs, empty chairs, roses, and daisies.

Name: ______________________________________

Age at time of death: _____ years ____ mos. _____ days

Parents' names: _______________________________

Where are they buried: _________________________

Symbols on their grave: ________________________

Epitaph: ____________________________________

Anything else to note: __________________________

____

____

Name: ____

Age at time of death: _____ years ____ mos. _____ days

Parents' names: ________________________________

Where are they buried: __________________________

Symbols on their grave: __________________________

Epitaph: ______________________________________

Anything else to note: ___________________________

____

____

Name: ______________________________________

Age at time of death: _____ years ____ mos. _____ days

Parents' names: ______________________________

Where are they buried: _________________________

Symbols on their grave: ________________________

Epitaph: ____________________________________

Anything else to note: _________________________

____

____

Name: ____

Age at time of death: _____ years ____ mos. _____ days

Parents' names: ________________________________

Where are they buried: __________________________

Symbols on their grave: __________________________

Epitaph: ______________________________________

Anything else to note: ___________________________

____

____

Name: ____

Age at time of death: _____ years ____ mos. _____ days

Parents' names: ________________________________

Where are they buried: __________________________

Symbols on their grave: __________________________

Epitaph: ______________________________________

Anything else to note: ___________________________

____

____

Name: ____

Age at time of death: _____ years ____ mos. _____ days

Parents' names: ________________________________

Where are they buried: __________________________

Symbols on their grave: _________________________

Epitaph: _______________________________________

Anything else to note: ___________________________

____

____

Name: ______________________________________

Age at time of death: _____ years ____ mos. _____ days

Parents' names: ______________________________

Where are they buried: _________________________

Symbols on their grave: ________________________

Epitaph: ____________________________________

Anything else to note: _________________________

____

____

Name: ______________________________________

Age at time of death: _____ years ____ mos. _____ days

Parents' names: ______________________________

Where are they buried: _________________________

Symbols on their grave: ________________________

Epitaph: ____________________________________

Anything else to note: _________________________

____

____

Name: ____

Age at time of death: _____ years ____ mos. _____ days

Parents' names: ______________________________________

Where are they buried: ______________________________

Symbols on their grave: _____________________________

Epitaph: ____

Anything else to note: _______________________________

____

____

Name: ______________________________________

Age at time of death: _____ years ____ mos. _____ days

Parents' names: ______________________________

Where are they buried: _________________________

Symbols on their grave: ________________________

Epitaph: ______________________________________

Anything else to note: __________________________

____

____

SKETCH A GRAVE

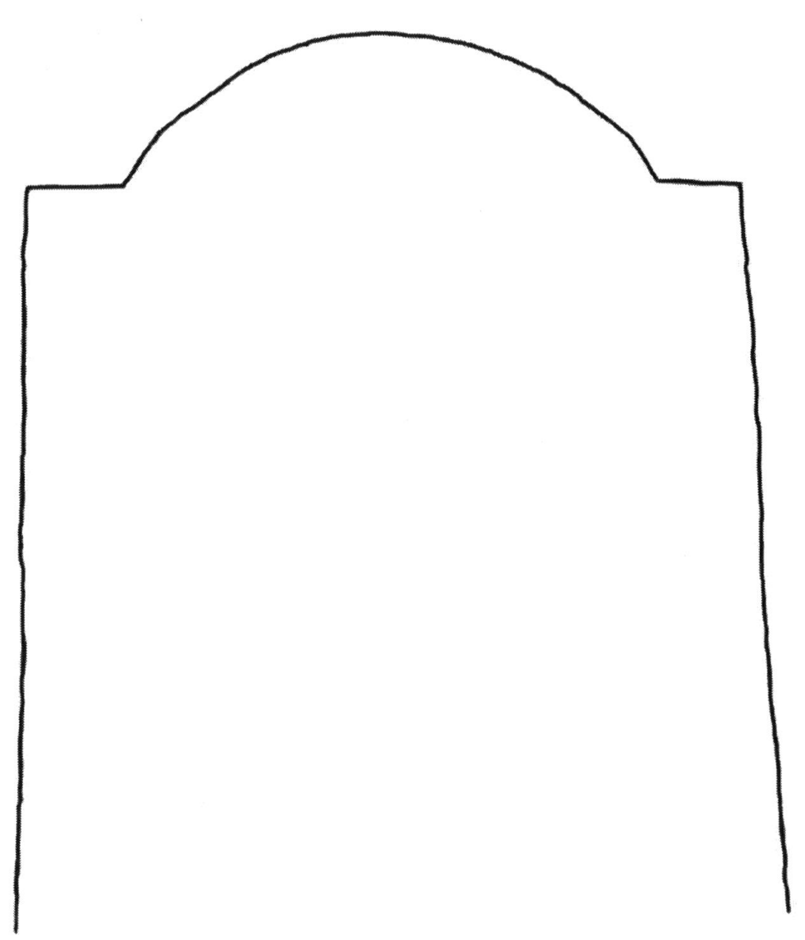

NOTES:

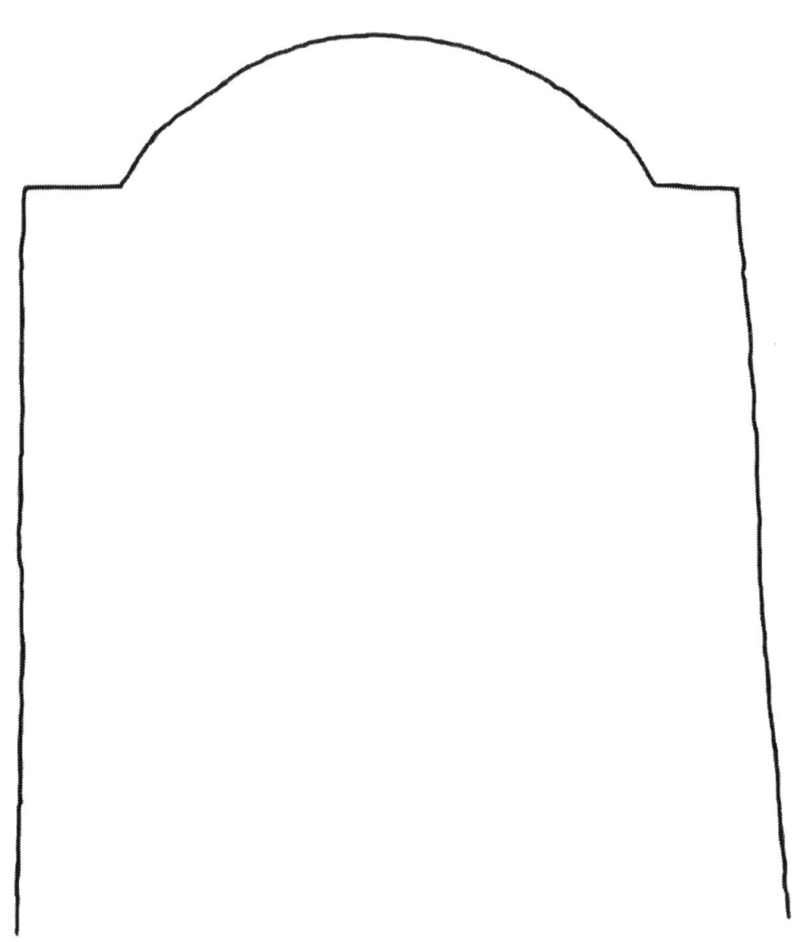

NOTES:

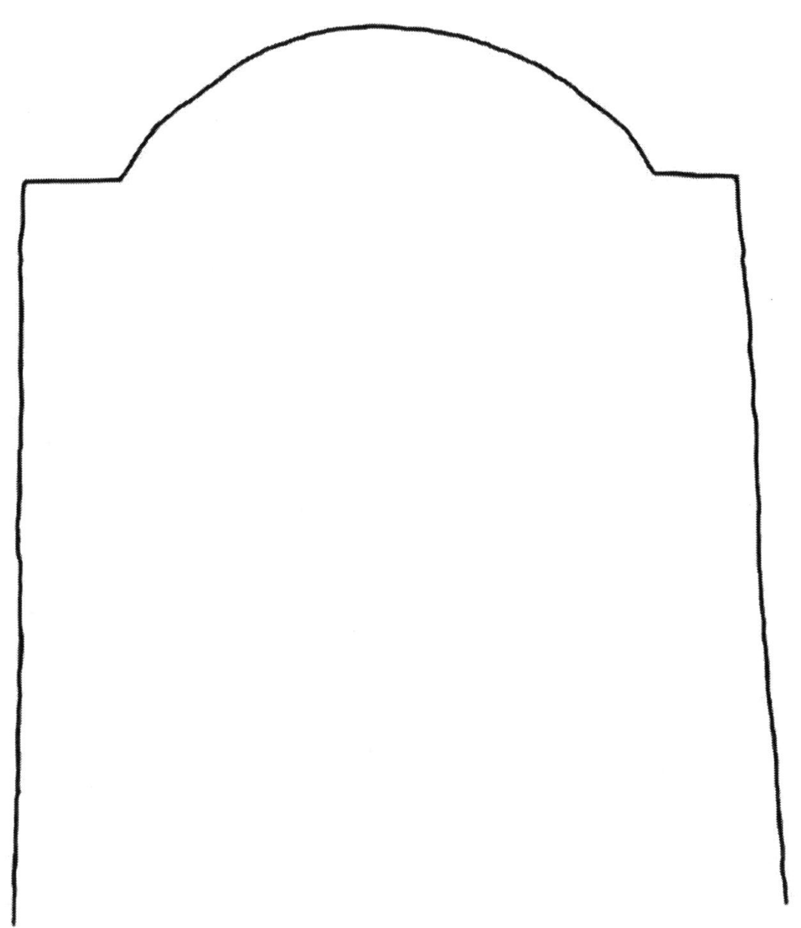

NOTES:

NOTES:

PERSONAL HISTORY

For many, exploring cemeteries is a way for them to research their genealogy. Whether this was your intention when you first began cemetery wandering or not, we hope you'll take the opportunity to fill out this section for your family members.

Ernest Hemingway said, "Every man has two deaths: when he is buried in the ground, and the last time someone says his name." We recommend using websites such as Ancestry and Family Search to try to get to know your ancestors better. By maintaining a familial bond and connection, we can keep their memory alive while also acquainting ourselves with both their lives and deaths.

The author's grandmother's grave ("Gramma Aw").

Name: ____________________ Relation: ______________

Married? Yes No Spouse's Name: ________________

Children? Yes No Children's Names: ______________

____

Occupation: ______________________________________

Cause of Death: ___________________________________

Epitaph? ____

Anything else to note? ____________________________

____

Use the space below to sketch an image of their grave or paste a photo of it to always keep with you.

Name: ____________________ Relation: ______________

Married? Yes No Spouse's Name: ________________

Children? Yes No Children's Names: ______________

____

Occupation: ______________________________________

Cause of Death: ___________________________________

Epitaph? ____

Anything else to note? _____________________________

____

Use the space below to sketch an image of their grave or paste a photo of it to always keep with you.

Name: ____________________ Relation: ______________

Married? Yes No Spouse's Name: ________________

Children? Yes No Children's Names: ______________

____

Occupation: ____________________________________

Cause of Death: _________________________________

Epitaph? ______________________________________

Anything else to note? ____________________________

____

Use the space below to sketch an image of their grave or paste a photo of it to always keep with you.

Name: ____________________ Relation: ______________

Married? Yes No Spouse's Name: ________________

Children? Yes No Children's Names: ______________

____

Occupation: ______________________________________

Cause of Death: __________________________________

Epitaph? ____

Anything else to note? ____________________________

____

Use the space below to sketch an image of their grave or paste a photo of it to always keep with you.

Name: ____________________ Relation: ______________

Married? Yes No Spouse's Name: ________________

Children? Yes No Children's Names: ______________

____

Occupation: ______________________________________

Cause of Death: ___________________________________

Epitaph? ____

Anything else to note? ____________________________

____

Use the space below to sketch an image of their grave or paste a photo of it to always keep with you.

CEMETERY BUCKET LIST

- ☐ Abraham Lincoln's grave
- ☐ Acanthus leaves
- ☐ Acorns and oak leaves
- ☐ Actor's grave
- ☐ Anchor
- ☐ Angel
- ☐ Anne Boleyn's grave
- ☐ Archway
- ☐ Author's grave
- ☐ Basket
- ☐ Bat
- ☐ Beehive
- ☐ Bench
- ☐ Bird
- ☐ Bob Marley's grave
- ☐ Bones
- ☐ Book
- ☐ Bud
- ☐ Bugle
- ☐ Burial mound
- ☐ Butterfly
- ☐ Cairn
- ☐ Calla lily
- ☐ Candle
- ☐ Cannon
- ☐ Cenotaph
- ☐ Chains
- ☐ Charles Darwin's grave
- ☐ Civil War veteran's grave
- ☐ Clock
- ☐ Clover
- ☐ Coffins
- ☐ Cohen hands
- ☐ Column

- [ ] Corn
- [ ] Crossbones
- [ ] Crown
- [ ] Curtains
- [ ] Daffodil
- [ ] Daisy
- [ ] Death's head
- [ ] Dog
- [ ] Double grave
- [ ] Drapery/Pall
- [ ] Elvis Presley's grave
- [ ] Empty chair
- [ ] Epitaph: Funny
- [ ] Epitaph: Sad
- [ ] Epitaph: Unique
- [ ] Eye
- [ ] Family member's grave
- [ ] Famous person's grave
- [ ] Father Time
- [ ] Fern
- [ ] Fieldstone
- [ ] Fish
- [ ] Forget-me-not
- [ ] Frank Sinatra's grave
- [ ] George Washington's grave
- [ ] Grapes
- [ ] Grave found in a movie
- [ ] Grave with a legend
- [ ] Grim Reaper
- [ ] Half-carved stone
- [ ] Hammer
- [ ] Hand holding flowers
- [ ] Hand of God
- [ ] Hand pointing down
- [ ] Hand pointing up
- [ ] Handshake
- [ ] Harp
- [ ] Harry Houdini's grave
- [ ] Hourglass
- [ ] IHS
- [ ] Imperial crypt
- [ ] Inverted torch
- [ ] Ivy
- [ ] Jane Austen's grave
- [ ] John Lennon's grave

- [ ] Key
- [ ] Lamb
- [ ] Lamp
- [ ] Lily
- [ ] Lily of the Valley
- [ ] Lion
- [ ] Lon Chaney's grave
- [ ] Lotus
- [ ] The Magnificent Seven
    - [ ] Abney Park
    - [ ] Brompton
    - [ ] Highgate
    - [ ] Kensal Green
    - [ ] Nunhead
    - [ ] Tower Hamlets
    - [ ] West Norwood
- [ ] Manus Dei
- [ ] Marilyn Monroe's grave
- [ ] Mark Twain's grave
- [ ] Marriage handshake
- [ ] Martin Luther King Jr's grave
- [ ] Mary Jane Kelly's grave (Jack the Ripper victim)
- [ ] Mason handshake
- [ ] Mass grave
- [ ] Mortsafe
- [ ] Mushrooms
- [ ] Musician's grave
- [ ] National Cemetery
- [ ] Obelisk
- [ ] Oddfellow chain
- [ ] Olive branch
- [ ] Oscar Wilde's grave
- [ ] Ossuary
- [ ] Owl
- [ ] Palm
- [ ] Pansy
- [ ] Passionflower
- [ ] Pentacle
- [ ] Pet Cemetery
- [ ] Poppy
- [ ] Portrait
- [ ] President's grave
- [ ] Primrose

- [ ] Pyramid
- [ ] Recipe on a grave
- [ ] Revolutionary War veteran's grave
- [ ] Rocks on a grave
- [ ] Rose
- [ ] Royalty's grave
- [ ] Salem Witch Trials Memorial
- [ ] Sarah Winchester's grave
- [ ] Sarcophagus
- [ ] Scroll
- [ ] Scythe
- [ ] Shell
- [ ] Ship
- [ ] Shovel
- [ ] Skeleton
- [ ] Skull
- [ ] Skull and crossbones
- [ ] Snake
- [ ] Soul effigy
- [ ] Square and compass
- [ ] Stars
- [ ] Statue of the deceased
- [ ] Sun
- [ ] Susan B. Anthony's grave
- [ ] Sword
- [ ] Sylvia Plath's grave
- [ ] Thistle
- [ ] Tree
- [ ] Tree stump
- [ ] Triple grave
- [ ] Tulip
- [ ] Urn
- [ ] Walt Disney's grave
- [ ] Weeping willow
- [ ] Wheat
- [ ] Wheel
- [ ] William Shakespeare's grave
- [ ] Winged Hourglass
- [ ] Wreath
- [ ] Zinker

Thy soul shall find itself alone
'Mid dark thoughts of the gray tombstone—
Not one, of all the crowd, to pry
Into thine hour of secrecy.

Be silent in that solitude,
Which is not loneliness—for then
The spirits of the dead who stood
In life before thee are again
In death around thee—and their will
Shall overshadow thee: be still.

—*Spirits of the Dead*
Edgar Allan Poe, 1827

FOLLOW AND SUPPORT THE MUSEUM

Scan the QR code below to find all our social media links, including our Patreon page, Facebook, Instagram, website, and merch shop.

100% of the money earned through our Patreon goes to expanding the museum, maintaining our current artifacts, and bringing the museum to various events around the country.

ACKNOWLEDGMENTS

This book is an ode and love letter to my grandmother, Gramma Aw. In her younger years, she loved taking her grandchildren on hikes throughout Western New York (but not before slamming on her brakes and getting all of us to pile out of her Jeep Wrangler to explore a countryside cemetery). As she got older, she knew she couldn't do such long drives and hikes, so she took us to Forest Lawn Cemetery in Buffalo instead. Each time she found an interesting monument or gravestone, she would excitedly call us over and make sure we took time to admire the artistry while also saying the deceased's name aloud. I am now doing the same thing with my son.

My friends and fellow taphophiles who contributed photos of graves that I could not track down myself: Vera Ahrweiler (@tombstone.tourism), Michele Baumann, Caroline Bennett, Amy and Ryan's Weird Adventures, Kari Bergen of Ephemera Obscura, Ivy Brandine, @cemetery_dryad, Diane E. Chambers, Darren and Jessica Cooke, Lizzie Craig, Rebecca Czyzewski (@kissing_the_shadows_666), Paige Dalton, Tara Feyko, Becki Fuller, Jacleen Gianaris, Katie Jo Glesing, Danielle "Verona Black" Gonzalez, Leah Griffiths, Leanna Renee Hieber, Jamie

Howells, Emma K. Isnor, Susan Jacobucci, Cedric Justice, Jasmine Kuzela, Ryan and Sam L., Elizabeth Martin, Stephanie Molnar, Amanda Montanari, Ryan and Shayna Muckerheide, Haiden Nelson, Amanda D. Paulson, Jay Rhoads (@m_t_graves), Mindi Ridgeway, Tracy Rose, Sharni (@urbanhaunts), Cindy Skawinski, Smell of Fear Candle Co., Vanessa Stipkovits, @to_the_graveyard_anais, and Ann Marie West.

The official patrons of my other death-related passion project: The Traveling Museum of Memento Mori. Through Patreon, these individuals financially back the museum's mission echoed in this book—to foster healthy conversations surrounding grief and death. Of those Patreon supporters, I want to give an extra special thanks to Kerri Collins, Carolyn Ernst Woomer, Brian Hogan, and Jim Sturgill.

As always, my little family—my mom and dad, husband, and son—who not only tolerate my morbid fascination with death but accompanied me on many cemetery excursions to make this book possible. All my love.

Last but not least: you, the reader. Thank you for picking up this book and thinking, *This one.* I hope you enjoyed exploring with it and it finds the perfect place in your spooky library.

RECOMMENDED READING

Arnold, Catharine. *Necropolis: London and Its Dead*. New York: Simon & Schuster, 2007.

Benoit, Tod. *Where Are They Buried: How Did They Die?* New York, NY: Black Dog & Leventhal Publishers, 2015.

Bouchard, Betty J. *Our Silent Neighbors: A Study of Gravestones in the Olde Salem Area*. Salem, MA: T.B.S. Enterprises, 2000.

Doughty, Caitlin, and Landis Blair. *From Here to Eternity: Traveling the World to Find the Good Death*. London: Weidenfeld & Nicolson, 2019.

Fury, Daniel. *If These Stones Could Speak: The History and People of the Old Salem Burying Point*. Salem, MA: Black Cat Tours Press, 2021.

Keister, Douglas. *Stories in Stone: A Field Guide to Cemetery Symbolism and Iconography*. Salt Lake City: Gibbs Smith, Publisher, 2004.

Rhoads, Loren. *199 Cemeteries to See Before You Die*. New York: Black Dog & Leventhal Publishers, 2017.

Ross, Peter. *Tomb with a View: The Stories and Glories of Graveyards*. Headline Book Publishing, 2021.

Slaughter, April, and Troy Taylor. *Disconnected from Death: The Evolution of Funerary Customs & the Unmasking of Death in America*. Jacksonville, IL: American Hauntings Ink, 2018.

Woomer, Amanda R. *The Art of Grieving: The Beauty Behind Victorian Mourning Customs*. Buffalo, NY: Spook-Eats Publishing, 2023.

Yalom, Marilyn. *The American Resting Place: 400 Years of History Through Our Cemeteries and Burial Grounds*. Boston: Houghton Mifflin Co., 2008.

REFERENCES

Adelman, Garry, and Timothy H Smith. "Lessons from the Fallen: Depictions of the Dead of Antietam." American Battlefield Trust, March 25, 2021. https://www.battlefields.org/learn/articles/lessons-fallen-depictions-dead-antietam#:~:text=Whistler%20of%20Company%20E%2C%20130th,all%20power%20of%20verbal%20expression%E2%80%A6.

City of London (England). Court of Aldermen. And City of London (England). Lord Mayor., 2007, Orders conceived and published by the Lord Major and aldermen of the city of London, concerning the infection of the plague, Oxford Text Archive, http://hdl.handle.net/20.500.12024/A53403.

"Grave Matters: St. Mary's Church Gardens." Let the Stones Speak, the Spire and Crypt Inspire, 2007. https://web.archive.org/web/20070814030528/http://www.stmaryislington.org/history/036.html.

"The Great Plague." Royal Museums Greenwich. Accessed November 3, 2023. https://www.rmg.co.uk/stories/topics/great-plague#:~:text=Bubonic%20plague%20terrorised%20Europe%20for,fifth%20of%20the%20city's%20population.

Hopkinsville Kentuckian. [volume] (Hopkinsville, Ky.), 7 July 1899. *Chronicling America: Historic American Newspapers*. Lib. of Congress. https://chroniclingamerica.loc.gov/lccn/sn86069395/1899-07-11/ed-1/seq-2/

"Industry Statistical Information." Cremation Association of North America. Accessed November 3, 2023. https://www.cremationassociation.org/page/IndustryStatistic.

"Life Expectancy and Healthy Life Expectancy." World Health Organization. Accessed November 3, 2023.

https://www.who.int/data/gho/data/themes/mortality-and-global-health-estimates/ghe-life-expectancy-and-healthy-life-expectancy#:~:text=Globally%2C%20life%20expectancy%20has%20increased,reduced%20years%20lived%20with%20disability.

Ridgway, Katherine. “Mortsafes.” Department of Historic Resources, April 27, 2021. https://www.dhr.virginia.gov/blog-posts/mortsafes/.

Ruiz, Teofilo F. *Medieval Europe: Crisis and Renewal*. Teaching Co., 1996.

Shipman, Pat Lee. “The Bright Side of the Black Death.” American Scientist, May 2, 2018. https://www.americanscientist.org/article/the-bright-side-of-the-black-death#:~:text=The%20epidemic%20killed%2030%20to,when%20the%20plague%20reached%20London.

The Weekly Exponent. (Peapack and Gladstone, N.J.), 08 March 1923. *Chronicling America: Historic American Newspapers*. Lib. of Congress. https://chroniclingamerica.loc.gov/lccn/sn88071052/1923-03-08/ed-1/seq-7/

ABOUT THE AUTHOR

Writer, anthropologist, and dark historian, Amanda R. Woomer was born and raised in Buffalo, NY. The owner of The Traveling Museum of Memento Mori, she is a featured writer for *Haunted Magazine*, *The Morbid Curious*, and the curator of the all-female paranormal journal, *The Feminine Macabre*. She is the author of 17 books for kids and adults, including *The Art of Grieving*, *A Very Frightful Victorian Christmas*, as well as *A Child's Guide to Cemeteries*. Follow her spooky adventures at spookeats.com and on Facebook, Instagram, and Twitter. To learn more about The Traveling Museum of Memento Mori, visit:

TravelingMuseumOfMementoMori.com

Made in the USA
Middletown, DE
02 February 2025

70018452R00199